We're not Selling, we're Winning.

We're not Selling, we're Winning.

The Simple Blueprint That Grew Our Practice From $280K to $4M

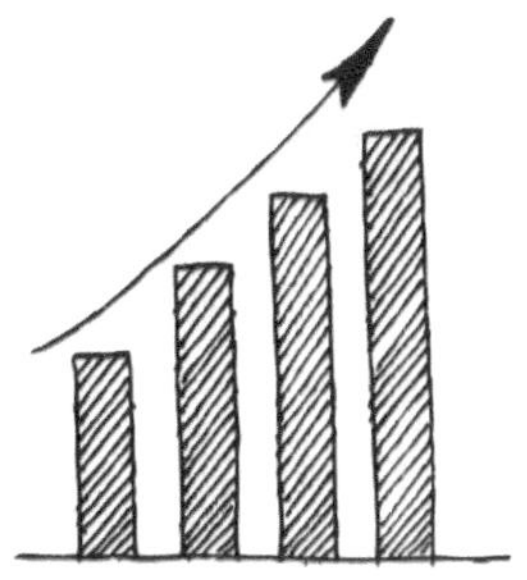

Kurt Steele

Visit the author's website at www.DrKurtSteele.com
Published and distributed by: STRONGPrint Publishing

We're Not Selling, We're Winning: The Simple Blueprint That Grew Our Practice from $280K to $4M

ISBN: 978-1-962074-28-5 Hardcover
ISBN: 978-1-962074-26-1 Paperback
ISBN: 978-1-962074-27-8 ebook

To my wife, Sacha.

When you marry the girl of your dreams,
all your other dreams seem possible.

Contents

Introduction

Thirty years ago, when I started in this profession, about 70–75% of optometry practices were independently owned. Doctors who went to optometry school could reasonably expect to own their own practice one day, build something meaningful, and maybe even pass it on to the next generation.

Today, that number has dropped to 40%. In just three decades, we have gone from owning 3 out of 4 of our practices to less than half of our practices being owned independently. And if we don't do something about it, that number is going to keep falling. This should concern every single optometrist out there, whether you're fresh out of school or you've been practicing for decades. Because the less we independently own our practices, the more at risk we are as a profession.

Over the last 30 years, I've seen independent practices get bought out by equity groups, swallowed up by corporate chains, and pushed out by ophthalmology groups. Most disheartening of all, I've seen many talented optometrists choose to work for these groups instead of taking the risk of ownership.

Now, I want to make one thing abundantly clear. Optometrists who work for ophthalmology groups, corporate chains, or equity-owned practices provide excellent care and we have great leaders in all three arenas. Lots of factors go into deciding where to work. Some optometrists may not want to own a business. Sometimes you are moving to a certain area and just need to take the best job available. People make decisions based on many factors, including what is best for them and their family. But as optometrists, it is in our best interest to preserve independent optometry in this country. Because when it comes to fighting for the future of our profession, nobody can advocate for optometry more than an independent business owner.

The reality is that if it were up to ophthalmology groups (especially the academy), we'd just do glasses, contacts, and nothing else. Optometrists in practices owned by equity groups have shareholders to answer to, not just their patients. And optometrists in corporate settings, while having lots of independence, also have a district manager or boss to answer to.

When you own your own practice, you don't have to answer to a shareholder, a corporate boss, or an ophthalmologist. You have the clearest, most direct stake in preserving and advancing the scope, respect, and independence of our profession. Independent practitioners have the most to gain and the most to lose based purely on the strength and autonomy of the optometric profession. When we advocate, we're advocating for the only thing we do—and that singular focus matters, especially in the political arena.

When independent optometry disappears, we lose our voice. We lose our ability to shape the future of our profession. We lose control over how we practice, how we serve our patients, and how we build our businesses. And eventually, we risk losing what makes optometry special in the first place.

I'm tired of seeing huge eye care clinics owned mostly by equity groups or ophthalmology groups. I'm tired of watching talented optometrists give up on the dream of practice ownership because they think it's too risky or too hard or because they simply don't know how to make it work. And I'm especially tired of watching independent practices struggle and fail when they don't have to.

That's where this book comes in.

My Mission

The core passion behind this book—my "why" for writing it—is simple: I want to provide a blueprint for independent optometrists to build thriving, multi-million dollar practices that can be passed on from generation to generation while staying independent.

I want this book to revolutionize independent optometry and get us on the rise again. I want to reverse that trend. I want to at least freeze that number at 40%, then watch it climb back up to 50% and beyond. I believe that's possible.

But here's the thing: it's not going to happen by accident. It's going to take work. It's going to take courage. And most importantly, it's going to take knowledge—the kind of knowledge they simply didn't have time to teach you in optometry school.

See, when I look at why so many independent practices struggle or fail, it's rarely because the optometrist isn't talented or doesn't care about their patients. It's because they were never taught how to run a business. They were taught how to be excellent doctors, but not how to build excellent practices.

They don't know how to hire and retain great team members. They don't know which metrics to track or how to use data to make confident decisions. They don't know how to talk to patients about technology that will improve their vision without feeling "salesy." They don't know when it's time to add another doctor or expand their space. And they certainly don't know how to do all of this while actually enjoying their life and not burning out.

That's exactly what this book is going to teach you.

When I took over my practice 30 years ago, we were doing $280,000 in annual revenue. We had three employees who we paid a dollar more than McDonald's, and we had constant turnover. I was doing everything myself—prepping patients, selecting frames, training contact lens wearers, and barely keeping my head above water.

Today, across two locations, we're approaching $4 million in annual revenue. I work an average of three days a week seeing patients. I have team members who have been with me for over 10 years, and one for over 25 years. We're building a new location that I expect will add another $3 million. And I genuinely love going to work every single day.

This was certainly not done alone. First of all, adding Dr. Emily Eisenhower to our Newport location is perhaps the best decision ever made in that location. She has continued the excellent standard set by our predecessors, Nathan, Bill, and Jeff. She has taken amazing care of our patients while becoming a great leader in our profession, already serving as Tennessee president!

Dr. Graham Taylor has also been amazing for our Greeneville location. Really, he could write his own book because he has taken that practice and grown to be very successful in his own way while building a great team. I can see why Jeff handpicked you, Graham! I am kind of bragging on myself—during a time when I often hear, "I can't find young doctors who want to come here and take ownership of a practice," I managed to get two extremely talented optometrists to join me in rural East Tennessee. It has gone well for all of us!

Every time you implement these strategies and grow your practice, you're proving that independent optometry works.

Every time you create a workplace where talented optometrists actually want to work, you're creating an alternative to corporate, equity, or ophthalmology employment. Every time you build something successful that you can pass on to the next generation, you're preserving the future of our profession.

The big chains, corporate groups, and equity firms aren't going away. But they don't have to dominate, either; they dominate when independent practices falter—when talented optometrists give up and take employed positions because practice ownership seems impossible.

When independent practices thrive, they provide amazing care, experiences, and outcomes. That's when we win and our patients win. That's when we prove that independent optometry isn't just surviving—it's thriving.

What You'll Gain From This Journey

I've had people telling me I should write a book for the better part of a decade. For a while, I thought they were just being nice. But the more my coaching work took off, the more I started to realize that *many,* if not *most,* optometrists were struggling with the same problems I once faced. Since I can't visit every optometry practice in the world, I figured a book would be the best way to help. So here we are.

This book contains the lessons I wish I had known when I first started my practice. It's about building a practice that works for you, not against you. It's about learning how to run a business and all the other real-world lessons I had to learn through years of research and a healthy dose of trial and error (which you now get to benefit from). Perhaps most importantly, it's about having the courage to make big changes.

This book is organized into three parts that build on each other—the information we cover in Chapter 1 supports Chapter 2, and so on and so forth. For that reason, it is best read from start to finish. That said, I know you are busy and you may not need *all* of the advice from each chapter. So feel free to skip around if you'd like—just be warned that I will be referencing content from previous chapters, which may cause some confusion at times.

In Part 1, we'll talk about your team. I've started the book here because this is the foundation for growth. Having a great team will get you very far, and it will make all your future efforts even more impactful. In the first three chapters, you'll learn how to hire the right people, pay them what they deserve, train them effectively, and lead them in a way that creates loyalty. Perhaps most importantly, you'll see why putting your team first actually leads to better patient care and higher revenue.

In Part 2, we'll dive into the metrics. I've spent the better part of two decades fine-tuning the metrics in my business, and now you get to learn all the tips and tricks I've learned along the way. I'll show you exactly which numbers to track, how to track them, and most importantly, how to use them as decision-making tools. You'll learn how to create budgets, implement bonus systems, know when to hire another doctor, and determine when it's time to expand your space. This is the stuff that separates struggling practices from thriving ones, and it's not nearly as complicated as you might think. Go to www. DrKurtSteele.com for downloadable resources so you can plug your numbers in and gain insights right away.

In Part 3, we'll cover how to talk to patients—or more specifically, how to NOT sell to them. In this part of the book, you'll learn how to build transformational relationships with your patients that create better outcomes for them and your practice. We'll cover specific verbiage and conversation strategies that will help you provide better care while increasing your revenue per exam. The best part? We're not selling anything to the patient—we're doing what's best for their eye health and vision.

Throughout the book, I'll share real examples from my own practice and all of the practices I've coached over the years. I'll show you the mistakes I've made so you don't have to make them yourself. And I'll give you practical, actionable systems you can implement immediately.

You're also going to hear a number of stories from my Dad, my senior practice partner, Dr. Jeff Foster, and many other important people in my life. I didn't get to where I am today on my own. In fact, I would be nowhere without those people. Hopefully, I can impart some of their wisdom to you through these stories. (They're also pretty great stories, if I don't say so myself!)

A Note on Faith

Psalm chapter 27:1 "The Lord is my light and salvation-whom shall I fear? The Lord is the stronghold of my life—of whom shall I be afraid?"

Before we dive in, I want to share something personal. I became a Christian later in life, getting baptized at age 53, and it fundamentally changed how I approach both life and business. At a few points, you'll see me reference my faith and how understanding that God is in control has given me the courage to make difficult decisions.

If that's not your thing, that's okay—the business principles in this book will work regardless of your spiritual beliefs. But for me, knowing that there's something bigger than myself out there, and that I'm ultimately in service to something greater, has made all the difference. It's taken the fear out of big decisions. It's helped me understand that taking care of my team and serving my patients well is about more than just building a business—it's about doing what's right.

When I realized that God wants me to have the energy to serve Him, to be there for my family, and to live a full life—not to grind myself into the ground—it changed everything. I started to see that working reasonable hours and taking care of my team isn't being lazy or uncommitted. It's being wise. It's being sustainable. And it's being faithful with what I've been given.

Let's Get Started

If it wasn't already abundantly clear, I wrote this book because I believe in independent optometry. I believe in you. And I believe that with the right knowledge and systems, you can build a practice that not only succeeds financially but also gives you the life you want to live.

We're not selling—we're building something better. We're keeping optometry independent.

Now let's get to work.

*Me, Dr. Foster, my Dad Steve, and my brother
Jason grimacing in Green Bay!*

Part 1
Your Team

1.

Making Courageous Decisions

In my work as a practice management coach, I've visited hundreds of optometry practices across the United States. When I first walk into an office, I always start with the same question: *"What's going well here?"*

9.99 times out of ten, I hear the same answers: "We put our patients first." "Our patients love us." "We take the best care of our patients." I'll hear the word "patients" thirty times before I hear anything about the doctor or their team. And that makes sense because as optometrists, we're trained to care for our patients and prioritize their health above all else. It certainly sounds like a good answer. We're supposed to put our patients first, right?

Well, that wouldn't be my answer. In my practice, I don't put my patients first—I put my team first. Always.

Now, don't get me wrong, we take excellent care of our patients. We realize that without patients our business doesn't exist, so it is in our best interest to give them the best possible experience. As you'll soon see, everything we do revolves around giving our patients the best possible care. We, as a team, do put our patients first. But *I,* as the owner of our practice, put my team first.

Why does this matter? Because these are the people I work with every day of my life. They're the ones who run the show, and I consider each one of them to be part of my family. By taking great care of my team, they, in turn, take great care of our patients. In fact, I would even say that our patients get *better* care because I take care of my team first. A great team with an amazing culture is a winning combination, every time.

I know it sounds counterintuitive, but it took me too long to learn this lesson, and it's one of many reasons why I'm writing this book. The key to a successful practice isn't just to prioritize your patients. You need to prioritize yourself, your team, and your patients—and maybe even just prioritize your team a little bit more. When you, as the owner, prioritize your team, your team will naturally prioritize your patients. It's a positive feedback loop that makes everything better. Life gets easier for you, work becomes more enjoyable for your team, and your patients get better care. (Oh, and your practice will grow!)

How do I know this? Because when I first started, I also put our patients above everything else. I spent years chasing patients and making decisions out of desperation—staying open later, opening on Saturdays, practically working myself (and my team) to the bone, all to serve our current patients and acquire new ones. Most of the decisions I made were through the lens of, "Is this better for our patients?", without considering my own needs or those of my team.

To be fair, that approach did work for a while. I grew our practice from $280,000 in revenue to about one and a half million by consistently putting our patients' needs above my own and those of my team, but I soon found myself hitting a wall. This is something I've now seen in many optometry practices around the country—you can get to a million by putting your patients first, but if you want to grow past that, you need a different approach.

This is how I operated for a long time, until a new approach came to me during a very dark period of my life. Within nine months, I lost three of the most important people in my world. I lost my younger brother, Jason, to kidney failure. Then my senior practice partner, Dr. Jeff Foster, to COVID. And finally, my dad, to ALS.

As I write this, I'm looking at a picture on my desk of the four of us in Green Bay. Dr. Foster's lifelong goal was to see the Packers play "in the blowing snow"—he wanted the full Green Bay experience, and boy did we get it. In that picture, the day before the game, it was negative four degrees with a wind chill of negative twenty. It might look like we're smiling, but those are grimaces. On the day of the game, it was twenty-two degrees—practically balmy in comparison—and it snowed six inches. We didn't care, and we had a blast that day. I'm really glad I went on that trip, because I'm the only one left alive in that picture.

Before they passed, I was like a hamster on a wheel, running myself (and my team) into the ground and trying everything I could to grow my practice. But those nine months put things into perspective for me. I realized life was too short to be obsessing over work and running myself ragged trying to build my business. I wanted to live a great life, and while I enjoyed optometry, there was so much more out there for me, and critically, my team.

I'll never forget the moment when it *really* hit me. I was standing outside the break room in our practice, and two of my team members were talking to each other. At the time, we were open till 7:00p.m. one night per week and until approximately 6:00p.m. another night of the week (to accommodate busy patients), and they were trying to decide who was going to miss their kids' baseball game that night as a result. It was one of those "I missed it last time, can you miss it this time?" conversations. Boy, did that crush me.

So I went right to my office manager, and I asked her how the evening hours were going. She told me that everyone hated them, that it was the *one* thing they didn't like about working at our practice. Right then and there, I told her to get rid of them, starting next week. The next day, we called and rescheduled all the evening appointments. This was the first of many changes I made to accommodate my team and put them first—and it was one of the best decisions I've ever made.

Here's the thing. We want our team to be efficient, and we want them to be great at their jobs so we can have a successful practice. But we also want them to be happy. We want our practice to be a fun, fulfilling place to work. Heck, we have to work here too! We now have a team that loves coming to work every day, and as a result, patients who love coming to our practice.

Did we lose some patients by cutting our hours? Probably. But now, we also get patients who drive forty miles for an eye exam just because our team is so good and it's such a pleasant experience to come into our office. I don't know about you, but I'd rather work with that patient than the one who's only coming in because our hours are convenient for them (and is causing my team to miss their kid's baseball games).

You know what else happened when I made those changes? We started to grow past that growth ceiling. Instead of being stuck at a million and a half, we've now grown to \$2.6 million in our current location and I anticipate it growing to \$3 million at least when we add another doctor in June. In just five years, our second location has grown from $400,000 to $1,400,000. It should become a $3 million practice after we complete our new building.

I'm not going to say that putting my team first was the sole reason for that growth. As you can imagine, that growth came from lots of work by lots of different people implementing systems and running our practice like a business—many of which we'll learn about in the following pages. But I can say that it was the start of a new direction for our practice. It was one of many tough decisions I've had to make in my practice.

As a business owner, you will be faced with many difficult decisions. In fact, most of what we'll talk about in this book is focused on giving you the courage to make tough decisions. You've probably noticed the word "courage" come up a few times already, and that's no coincidence. So before we get into the specifics on how to build and lead your team, I'd like to spend some time with that word. Because if this book can give you courage, everything else will work itself out.

A Note on Courage

Out of everything we'll cover in this book, I believe there is actually one overarching thing that is holding back 99% of optometrists. It is simply the fear of failure.

One of my favorite sayings is that "most limitations are self-imposed," and I like to add a second part, which is that *those self-imposed limitations are usually based in fear.* Most optometrists who hit a growth ceiling are held back because of some type of fear—fear of failure, fear of what patients might think, fear of spending money, fear of making a big change, and so on. These are the things that keep optometrists stuck, not a lack of knowledge or ability.

Now, I define **courage** in a few ways. The first is *doing the right thing when nobody's watching, or even when it might have negative consequences.* The second is *doing what's required to be successful in the face of fear.* Courage is the key to moving beyond fear and making the big decisions required to move your practice forward.

And here's the thing: you already have courage! It took courage just to go into private practice to begin with. It takes courage to own a business, period! I know that you already have courage within you, so my goal with this book is to help you harness that courage and use it to grow past whatever level you're at now.

See, for most of my life, I was the exact opposite of courageous. I grew up thinking it was best not to be heard. I was shy, afraid to speak up, afraid to take risks, and afraid to believe I was as good as anybody else. The smallest things would crush me.

This was how I lived my life for a long time, until one moment in optometry school when something changed. I was standing in a clinic getting chewed out by my professor for something, and normally that would have ruined my entire day. But something in me snapped that day, and I remember thinking, "I'm not going to let this guy ruin my day anymore." In that moment, I decided that I was done being shy and afraid. I was going to stand up for myself because I was as good as anybody and I was in control of my future.

That was a pivotal moment for me, and since then, I have gone from one extreme to the other. Today, I'm probably the least afraid person you'll ever meet, but it's not because I'm reckless. It's because I have the knowledge—and often the data—to make calculated decisions that I am confident in. It's a lot easier to be courageous when you know things are going to work out, and that's the type of courage I want you to walk away from this book with.

There's an old saying from a pastor named Charles Swindoll: "Life is 10% what happens to you and 90% how you react." I think that is so true. Most people go through life thinking this is more like a 50/50 ratio. They walk through life waiting for good things to happen to them or feeling bad about things that haven't worked out for them. Don't believe me? Just go on social media. People love to get on Facebook and complain about what they can't control. If they spent half the energy they use complaining about what they can't control and put it toward the 90% they can control, they'd be in much better shape.

Yes, there will be things in life that you can't control—but you can *always* control how you react. I actually think if you can get to that 90/10 split, you're doing pretty well. But really, you should be shooting for 99/1. If you ask me, life is really 1% what happens and 99% how you react. And it is not worth your time or effort to sit around and complain about the 1% or 10% of life you can't control.

In business, it might feel like there are a lot of things that are outside of your control. Well, I'm here to tell you that you have far more control than you think, and taking control all starts with courage. Courage is about doing what's required to be successful in the face of fear. That becomes a lot easier when you *know* exactly what's required to be successful, and that is the type of courage we are going to build together in this book.

People often tell me that I look at things differently, that I somehow make complex business decisions seem simple. But *it really is simple* when you have a great team behind you, when you have the right systems in place, and when you can make decisions based on data. It becomes easy to be courageous when you get good at measuring and projecting things, because you're no longer guessing or hoping things will work out.

If you're thinking "I'm not a numbers person," or "I'm not very risk-averse," don't worry. I know you have the ability to do this. When I look back at all the doctors I've coached over the years, it's not that they didn't know what to do. They had the knowledge and they had the courage. They were afraid because they didn't have the data to back up those decisions. They were making choices in the dark, and that's terrifying.

Even when I look back at the mistakes I've made in my practice, they were nearly all a result of fear, not lack of knowledge. It was probably the same fears you're having right now: fear of failure, fear of what patients might think, fear of spending money, or fear of making a big change. But once I put my faith in God and started making decisions based on data, with a solid plan to back me up, everything changed.

My mom had a saying that I heard a thousand times growing up: "Can't never could." She never let me say I couldn't do something. If I ever said "I can't," she'd immediately shut it down. In her eyes, it was simple—if you say you can't do something, you probably won't ever do it. You're defeating yourself before you even start.

My mom was my biggest cheerleader. She never discouraged me from anything—ever. She believed I could do whatever I set my mind to, and she made sure I believed it, too. And you know what? That made all the difference.

That is what this book is really about. All of the information, systems, and strategies we're going to talk about have one thing in common: they are designed to give you the courage to transform your practice into whatever your ideal vision is. You already have the ability to do this, you just need to take fear out of the equation. That's what we'll do together.

Building the Foundation

Your team is the foundation of everything else we're going to discuss in this book. All the metrics, systems, and strategies are not going to move the needle for you if you don't have the right people in place who genuinely care about your practice.

How do I know this? Well, I can tell you it's true from my own experience, but I've also seen the same trends in practices throughout the country. When I visit a new practice, one of the first things I do is send out an anonymous survey to the entire team. I'll ask them what's working, what's not working, and what needs to change. In many of those offices, I'll get responses like "We don't feel listened to," "We don't feel appreciated," and "We just want to be heard."

The interesting part is that in these cases, the doctors almost always think everything is fine. They aren't even thinking about their team because they have "bigger" things on their mind. They want to talk to me about marketing strategies and metrics and improving efficiency—the team is usually one of the last things on their mind. Yet here is their team, telling me they feel undervalued, overworked, or ignored. In many cases, they're coming to me with things that are broken or brilliant ideas that would benefit the practice! Yet the owner is completely unaware.

Let me tell you, if that's the case in your practice, then it is the number one problem you need to solve. When I look at the practices that are struggling to grow, stuck at a revenue ceiling, or experiencing high turnover, it almost always comes back to team issues. The doctor is talented, the patients are there, but the foundation is cracked. And you can't build a multi-million dollar practice on a cracked foundation.

Sometimes, doctors will even be aware of problems with their team, but in their eyes, it's the team's fault, not theirs. I'll hear things like "They just don't listen," or "We have a culture problem," or "Some people just aren't motivated." As the leader, your team is your responsibility. Their performance is dictated by your performance as a leader, and you need to be tuned into what is happening with the people in your business.

In the next two chapters, we're going to get into the specifics—how to hire people who will thrive in your practice, how to pay them in a way that makes financial sense, how to train them effectively, and how to lead them with a style that builds loyalty instead of resentment. We'll cover systems for accountability, strategies for dealing with negativity, and the exact framework I use to create a culture where people genuinely want to work hard.

But before we get into any of those specifics, let me make one thing abundantly clear: **Your team comes first.** Always. If you have their back, they'll have yours.

Key Takeaways

1. **You (as the owner) need to prioritize your team.** The most important mindset shift you can make is putting your team first, even above your patients. Their performance is dictated by your performance. As the leader of your practice, your team is your number one responsibility—they are the foundation that will make everything else work. If you have their back, they'll have yours.

2. **Prioritizing your team improves patient care.** When you put your team first, your patients actually receive better care. A happy, well-trained, appreciated team creates experiences that make patients drive forty miles past other optometrists. They're more attentive, more engaged, and more invested in patient outcomes because they're invested in the practice's success. It's a positive feedback loop that benefits everyone.

3. **Courage is the key to everything.** Most optometrists know what they should do, but fear holds them back. Fear of failure, fear of spending money, fear of what might go wrong. Courage is doing what's required to be successful in the face of that fear. And courage becomes a lot easier when you have the right systems, the right data, and the right team backing you up. Everything we'll cover in this book is designed to give you the knowledge and confidence to make courageous decisions.

2.
Building Your Team

____

When I first started at my current practice back in 1995, we had a simple hiring strategy that I'm almost embarrassed to admit to you now. We would figure out what McDonald's was paying, and pay one dollar an hour more than that.

We had three people working for us at that time, and two of them were making something like $6.50 an hour while the third was at minimum wage (which I think was $4.25/hour). We had two employees, Annette and Judy, who were underpaid but stayed out of loyalty. The third position was constant turnover, either because they weren't performing as they should or they found a better-paying job elsewhere. This went on for three years, and it was just miserable.

At one point, we had just lost another great employee, and I finally went to my senior practice partner, Jeff, and I said, "Look, we're never going to grow if we don't set our sights a little higher." See, there's a very simple rule in optometry, and it's something I have built my whole practice around: *you make money by seeing patients.* There is no activity that will provide a higher return on your time than seeing patients, plain and simple. And this is what was on my mind when I went to Jeff that day.

At that time, we saw about one patient per hour. I was doing everything—I was the tech, I did the frame selection, the contact lens training, and the insertion and removal. I was not good at this, by the way. I think about half the glasses wearers in Newport, Tennessee, had the same round tortoise shell frame because I just picked it for everyone. I don't even know why we had a frame board, we could have just had that one frame sitting there, since that's what everyone got.

I said to Jeff, "I don't even know why Annette and Judy are still here." (These were the two employees who were making a dollar more than McDonald's.) Annette was making even less in reality because she would take insurance claims home and fill them out at night with a typewriter. I paid her a salary of $270 a week for that, which practically makes me sick now.

It was clear that something needed to change, so we made the decision to give them raises—big ones. We threw out the McDonald's philosophy and decided that if we were ever going to grow this practice, we'd need to start investing in our team. Not just paying them well, but giving them more responsibility and training them to take over tasks that we didn't need to be doing so we could spend more time with patients.

I will never forget the conversation I had with Annette the day after Jeff and I made that decision. I went to her and I said, "Annette, we're giving you a raise." I literally increased her pay by 50%. But I went on to tell her that with that increased pay, she was going to take on some new responsibilities. I told her, "You're going to learn how to adjust glasses and order my contact lenses for me and do insertion and removal training" (among other things). I had a similar conversation with Judy.

Annette ended up working with me for almost 20 years. She became our office manager and fondly referred to herself as my "East Tennessee Mama." She passed away on December 17th, 2021—almost exactly one year after my dad passed away on December 16th, 2020—and I had the honor of helping give her eulogy. Annette was more than just a coworker; she was a lifelong friend and the foundation of our practice. I can say with 100% confidence that our practice would not be what it is today if it weren't for Annette—I miss her every day.

That conversation with Annette was the beginning of a new philosophy of mine: if you invest in people who invest in you, you create loyalty that money can't buy. The first person I hired with this new philosophy has now worked for me for 25 years. I hired her during an eye exam—if I remember correctly, she was about a +6.00-4.00X030. This was in the days of Sunsoft quarterly replacement lenses, back when you couldn't even get that kind of prescription in monthlies or dailies. Does anyone remember that? No? Just me?

Well, I kept forgetting to order them for her. I'm a very scattered person, so I'd forget or order the wrong thing. This patient, Amie, never got mad—she was just the nicest person. I could tell she was organized, and I enjoyed being around her. One day, it occurred to me that she would be a great person to work with.

"Amie, where do you work?" I asked.

"Dollar General."

"What do you do there?"

"I'm a cashier."

"What do you make, if you don't mind me asking?"

She told me. I offered her a good bit more, then said, "and that way you can order your own dang contacts!"

She laughed at me. I told her I was serious. That was over 25 years ago, and she still works with me to this day. The lesson? You can find great talent in unusual places, and the best way to bring that talent to your practice is to make it a win-win for you and them.

Keeping the Doctor in the Exam Room

Hiring and retaining employees is one of the most common pain points I hear from optometrists around the country, and it's something I dealt with for a long time. If you're reading this book, chances are you've dealt with those pain points too. Now, it's a little more complicated than just paying more on a whim—in a few pages, I'll explain to you the math behind those decisions and why they made sense—but the reality is that investing in your team is the best way to scale your practice because you cannot (and should not) do everything yourself.

If you are the "chief everything officer" right now and you're struggling to grow your practice or you're burning out from long hours, then this might be a sign that you need to rethink some things. *As an optometrist, the amount of time you spend in the exam room directly correlates to the amount of revenue you generate.* That also means that every minute you spend outside the exam room is lost income. Therefore, the simple solution to growing your practice is to delegate everything outside of the actual exams themselves.

This is not a new concept in optometry, but many practice owners still struggle to delegate certain tasks or are missing opportunities to take things off their plate. My senior practice partner, Dr. Foster, for example, was as old school as it gets. He knew the value of delegation but he still had many opportunities to improve.

For a long time, he was very against seeing more than two patients per hour, but I knew he could do more if we were more efficient. So I had him measure the amount of time he actually spent in the exam room examining or talking to the patient. He was syrupy slow and loved getting into long conversations with patients, but even then, it only took him 18 minutes to do a full exam and 12 minutes to do a follow-up exam. The reason he was seeing only two patients per hour is that he was spending five minutes leaving the room to find something, or another five updating their chart, billing, or coding.

Now, Dr. Foster would never have seen four patients an hour—that would've been too much for him because he wanted to be able to chat with his patients and he wanted some time to relax between exams. But when I showed him the numbers, he started to see what I was seeing. For every hour he was at our practice, he was really only spending 30 minutes with patients. So if we could figure out how to take away all that other stuff that was wasting his time, he could easily be doing three patients per hour while still spending the same amount of time, giving the same level of care, and taking some time to relax between patients. That simple change transformed his productivity and subsequently our revenue—and that decision became easy for both of us when we had the data to back it up.

Improving the efficiency of your team means you'll have more time to either see more patients, spend more time with each patient, or a combination of both. It's worth noting that there should be a balance here. You don't always want to max-imize the number of patients you can see per hour. If you're seeing too many, you're probably not giving them enough time, meaning it will be difficult to build a great relationship with them and you may be missing out on properly educating your patients. If you're seeing too few, you're wasting your time and leaving money on the table. We'll cover more details on this when we talk about performance metrics in Chapter 4, but for the most part, every optometrist should be focused on spending as much time in the exam room as possible.

So, how can you do that? It's simple, really—build a great team that can handle just about everything else in your business so all you have to do is see patients. This isn't about rushing patients or spending less time examining them; it's about being strategic with your time. When you can delegate effectively, you can actually see more patients per hour while spending as much or even more time with each of them!

In my experience, most optometrists know this but fall short of doing anything about it. They might still do a handful of tasks in their business because they feel it saves them money by not having to hire an additional employee. Or maybe they like doing accounting, so they still manage their own books (just kidding, that's never happened). Most commonly, however, they don't have the courage to trust their team. They don't feel comfortable delegating tasks they've been doing themselves for years. They feel that they are the only one who knows how to do it the "right way," and that having a member of your team do it is too risky.

That type of thinking will only hold you back. If you want to grow your practice, you have to prioritize delegating as much as possible so you can spend more time in the exam room with your patients. That's how you maximize your profitability. And the key to delegating, of course, is to have a great team that you trust.

Which brings us to the main topic of this chapter: Building your team. Building a great team is actually not as difficult as you might think. Really, it comes down to a few key steps:

Step 1: Hire the right people
Step 2: Pay them what they deserve
Step 3: Trust them!

Whether you're just getting started or you've been practicing for decades, these three strategies should help you build a team that can take things off your plate, so you can spend more time doing what you're best at and what makes you money.

What does this actually look like in practice? It means that your team is handling just about everything outside of giving the eye exam itself. When you walk into the exam room, all the preliminary work is done, and when that door opens again, your team takes care of everything else. One simple way to think about this is that if it doesn't require an optometry license, you should teach someone else how to do it.

As we all know, your team should be taking care of all the optical work, contact lens training, and pre-testing. These are all technical skills that can be taught. Most optometrists already have these basics in place. You probably already have an optical team and staff that takes care of contact lens training, for example. But really, that's just the bare minimum—if you train your team right, you can get to a level of efficiency where all you need to do is sit down in the exam room and start talking to the patient. Literally.

When I walk into the exam room, for example, the data has already been collected—but the room is also set up so that I don't even have to move around or look for anything. Their old prescription or the automated prescription reading is already in the phoropter. I don't have to dial it in. We have an AI system that records what I say to the patient, and that's already up and running. The patients' favorite dry-eye drop is already sitting out, so I don't have to walk over to the closet to get it. It might sound negligible, but a minute here and a minute there adds up. I've trained my techs to handle everything they possibly can so that when I open that door, all I have to do is sit down and start the exam.

I know you already know this, but it's worth a reminder. Your team should be trained (and sometimes retrained) to handle just about everything so you can focus on what you do best—interpreting data, problem solving, and building relationships with your patients. And that goes beyond the exam room, too. You shouldn't be having to spend your time handling HR complaints or making purchasing decisions—those are all things that should be delegated to your team. This doesn't just save you time; it means better care for your patients and more revenue for your practice.

So, with all that in mind, let's start with Step 1. Hiring good people is one of the biggest challenges optometrists face, and I will tell you it's easier than you think. It's all about identifying talent—wherever you might find it.

Hiring the Right People

I have three simple rules when it comes to hiring:

1. I only hire happy people.
2. I don't hire out of need, I hire out of want.
3. I don't care about experience.

I know this might sound crazy, but it works. I've gone the traditional hiring route—I've posted the applications, done the interviews, checked references, and hired experienced people—and none of those people are still at my practice. Every employee who is still at my practice was hired based on those three rules.

One of my favorite hiring stories comes from a Waffle House in my hometown of Newport, Tennessee. Now, before I tell the story, let me just say this. If you've ever gone to a business repeatedly because *a specific person* works there, you should probably hire that person. Patty was one of those people.

The Waffle House in Newport was the second-highest-grossing Waffle House in the state of Tennessee. For those that don't know, Waffle House is a diner that is open 24 hours a day, seven days a week, and there are 142 Waffle Houses in Tennessee alone. I am confident that Patty was the reason for this Waffle House's success. I went to that Waffle House *because of Patty,* and I know I wasn't the only one.

I can remember sitting in that Waffle House one day, eating an omelet, when this guy came in. He looked rough, as if he had just walked off the set of Duck Dynasty, and he was pissed. I can't remember exactly what he was mad about, but he looked like he was about to blow up at the first person who stepped in front of him. I remember thinking, "Holy crap, I hope he doesn't have a gun."

When he walked through the door, you could see all the employees look at him, then look at Patty as if to say, "You do something." Patty was the leader, even though she wasn't the manager, and she had an uncanny ability to make any customer happy. It was remarkable, like nothing I had ever seen. She met that guy at the door, and within two minutes, he was laughing and smiling. I had seen enough.

The next time she came by my table, I said, "Hey Patty, how long have you been working here?"

"21 years," she said.

"Do you like working here?"

"You know, it's funny you ask that, because I've been working here for a long time and I've been starting to wonder if it's time to do something else."

I asked the question. "Well, what do you make?"

She didn't know exactly what she was making since it was tip-based, but whatever number she gave me, I told her I'd pay her three dollars more.

It took her a second, and she clearly didn't believe me, so I told her, "I'm not kidding. I'm serious. Just let me finish eating and get out of here though, because they're going to be pissed—but I would like to hire you."

She told me she didn't have experience working in this type of environment. I told her I didn't care. I hired Patty because she was a happy person, and I wanted her to work for me. When I look back at my staff, the four people who have been here for ten years or more were all hired out of want, not need. But they're all good people, and good people make you money.

So the first day Patty came here, Annette, who was our office manager at the time, asked what we were going to do with her.

I told her, "I don't care. Make her the Director of Smiles."

She actually was the Director of Smiles for a few months. I told her, "Patty, we have 9,400 square feet here—all you have to do is walk around and make everybody feel like they felt when they came into that Waffle House. Offer them water, tell them why we're ten minutes behind, and maybe learn a few things so you can help out where we need help. But you're the Director of Smiles, and that's all I care about. If you just make people feel like they felt when they came into Waffle House, you're doing what I hired you for."

We actually got some new patients from hiring Patty. They would go to Waffle House and ask where Patty was. Someone would tell them, "Oh, that eye doctor hired her," and then they'd come in to see her and get an eye exam. I'm not kidding.

When I look at my staff, both current and past, the ones that have stayed more than 5 years are the ones I've hired out of want, not need. I once hired a woman named Candace from Krystal, which is a fast-food burger restaurant similar to White Castle. I liked to get the Sunrisers from Krystal and take the sausage and cheese off the bun (low carb). I remember going through the drive-thru at Krystal and seeing Candace a few times, and her smile just lit up the room (or the drive-thru window, I suppose). I asked her if she would consider working for me, and she worked with me for four years.

My brother Jason knew both Patty and Candace, and let's just say that Waffle House and Krystal both get a lot of late-night guests. He once remarked, "You just get drunk and hire people!" While that's not true, I'll admit it doesn't look great. For the record, I was just getting a normal meal at both places—those weren't late nights.

Now, one thing about hiring good people is that you will lose them sometimes. Candace was a successful hire, and she did a great job working with us, but she ended up leaving us because she wanted to go into cosmetology. She is now a very successful cosmetologist, and I think that's fantastic. When she told me she was leaving to pursue that, I was so happy for her—and I'd like to think that working in our practice set her up for that next leap.

If you ask me, part of your role as an employer is to help people develop their skills. If you hire a good person and they end up leaving later on because they're moving on to bigger and better things, that's a win in my book. You've helped them and they've helped you. What's important is that people aren't leaving for the wrong reasons, like your culture or policies.

The moral of the story is that good people help you grow, and good people can be found in all sorts of places.

The Anti-Experience Philosophy

If you were to survey every hiring manager, entrepreneur, and business owner around the world and ask them the number one quality they look for in a candidate, what do you think it would be? My hunch is that "experience" would be number one on that list, or at least in the top three.

That just doesn't make any sense to me. The main problem with hiring an experienced person is that they are leaving their current practice for one reason or another. If they didn't like the previous eye clinic they worked at, they're probably not going to like yours either.

The other problem with hiring experienced people is that they tend to be stuck in their own ways. They learned how to work in a certain way at their previous job, and they're going to want to work that way at your practice, too. Have you ever heard an employee say something like, "Well, at my last job, we did it this way"? I'll bet you have, and that's typically not a great thing for you or your team to deal with. Those types of people can be challenging to work with because they're resistant to change. Having to break those habits is not only inefficient, it can also affect team morale if they're complaining about how things are done or telling everyone how their last clinic did it.

I'd almost always rather hire a good person with little to no experience and train them *my way* than have to re-train someone who already has experience working at a different practice. In later chapters, you'll see that we tend to do things a bit differently at my practice, and we have systems to train people. It doesn't really matter how much experience you have; if you're joining our practice, you're going to be trained on our systems, so starting from scratch is often easier and more effective than breaking old habits.

This also brings up another topic, which is that I never make business decisions based on what my competition is doing. My dad always said, "If you only pay attention to your competition, you can only be as smart as your dumbest competitor." What I took from that is that you should always focus on setting your own standard and doing what's best for your practice, rather than trying to do what someone else is doing.

I set my own standard for our practice, and it is very high. Frankly, I don't know what standards my competitors set, and I'm not really concerned about what they're doing.

Now, that's not to say that I won't take great ideas when I see them. Over the years, I've been lucky enough to work with a lot of successful practices, and I'll be the first to admit that I'll steal great ideas from them when I see them. Just ask my team—I can't tell you how many times I've come back to the office after visiting a practice and I'll be all excited to tell them about a great new idea. I learned. Some of the ideas in this book come from practices I've coached, and I've given credit where credit is due.

The point being, if you compare yourself to average, you'll end up average. Set your own standard, do what's best for your practice, and there's nothing wrong with stealing a great idea when you see it.

Paying Your Team Well

The second step in building a great team is to pay them well. This, of course, applies to people when you hire them, but it also applies to your current employees.

At the beginning of this chapter, I mentioned how I increased Annette's salary significantly. That might have sounded crazy, but it actually made perfect sense on paper.

Remember, the goal is to keep the doctor in the exam room. When you break down the numbers, giving an employee a raise can actually make you money—*if* it is accompanied with more responsibilities, of course. Here's how I think about it.

Let's say you give someone on your team a two-dollar-per-hour raise. That's equivalent to an extra $16 per day ($2 x 8 hours). Now, let's say you generate an average of $400 in revenue per exam. If that raise means you can do just one more exam per day, you're profiting $384 more per day. If you can do two more exams, that's $784 per day. Even if it only results in one more exam *per week,* you're still profiting $320 per week! That's a no-brainer.

If you're having trouble delegating to your team or you're stuck spending too much time outside of the exam room, then giving raises to your current team and expecting more might be a great way to move things forward.

And while you could just ask your team to do more for the same pay, I wouldn't exactly recommend that. When you do that, they're going to feel like you're ordering them to do more with no real reason behind it. They were hired to do a certain set of tasks; why should they all of a sudden have to do more with no difference in pay?

When you present them with a raise, however, that changes the conversation. Instead of ordering them to do more, you're asking them if they would be open to taking on more responsibility in exchange for more money. I like to even take it a step further by asking them if they would prefer a raise with some additional responsibilities, or if they are maxed out and would like to hire more help instead. I involve them in the decision.

Now, most people are going to take the raise. Not only are they making more money, but they're moving up in their career! They're learning new skills, and that's important. In fact, just look at the top 10 factors of job satisfaction (from a survey of over 200,000 people by the Boston Consulting Group):

1. Appreciation for your work
2. Good relationships with colleagues
3. Good work-life balance
4. Good relationships with superiors
5. The company's financial stability
6. Learning and career development
7. Job security
8. Attractive fixed salary
9. Interesting job content
10. Company values

Giving someone a raise in exchange for taking on additional responsibilities hits on six out of those ten factors. You're telling them you appreciate their work (#1), likely improving your relationship with them (#4), providing an opportunity for them to learn and develop in their career (#6), ensuring they have job security (#7)—because why would you give them a raise if you're about to let them go?—offering an attractive salary (#8), and making their day-to-day more interesting (#9). What's not to like about that?

The key is how you make this happen. If you're hiring a new person, you'll want to think about what they should be responsible for from the get-go, and then explain to them how their rate is reflective of that. When it comes to your current team, the conversation is similar. The key is to show them that you value their work and make it clear that you're willing to pay them more if they're willing to take on some more responsibilities—or if that's not feasible, then that money can go toward hiring additional help.

So, what happens next? Well, assuming they're up for taking on those additional responsibilities, you need to set them up for success! And that happens through training.

Trust Through Training

Here's something I've learned after 30 years in this business: If somebody's not performing well, it's almost always a result of training, rather than a problem with the person themselves. In my coaching work, optometrists often tell me they can't trust their team with certain tasks. My next question is always, "Well, how much have they been trained?" I'm usually met with a blank stare or I find out they were trained once several years ago. When you are the boss or manager, you have to be a parrot. You will have to repeat yourself! How often did you hear something or learn something one time, and that's all you needed? It takes repetition for someone to learn something. There is an old adage of advertising—someone needs to hear something at least five to seven times before it even takes hold. So, yes, you have to repeat yourself.

If you're having a problem with your team or you don't trust them, that's more of a "you" issue than a "them" issue. A good leader shoulders the blame. Look at the mistakes they make and ask yourself, is it your fault or their fault? Most people do the best they can with the tools they have and the training you've given them, so if you're running into performance problems or you can't trust your team, it's probably because you haven't set them up for success with adequate training.

When someone on my team isn't performing well, I always ask our office manager, Molly, how they've been trained. More often than not, we'll find that their training was a bit lackluster, or that it happened a long time ago, or that maybe some things have changed since they were last trained, and we need to update our system.

Training is not something that you can do once and never again. One way I like to think of it is to imagine a football team that never practices. They just show up every weekend for the game, and that's it. How do you think they'd perform?

The best sports teams don't just stop practicing during the regular season. They keep practicing in between games. They keep working on the fundamentals. They're always focused on improving. If they start skipping practices, they're going to get sloppy.

Your team is no different! For us, seeing patients is game time. If you want to have a high-performing team, you can't expect to just play games and get better, or even stay the same. You need to keep practicing and working on the fundamentals. It has to be scheduled in, and it has to be consistent.

Cross-Training

In my practice, we spend what some might consider an unusual amount of time cross-training so that everybody can help everybody. This is helpful in the event that someone can't come in, in which case another person can take over their responsibilities for the day. But it's also helpful because if someone runs into a problem, they can just ask their coworkers before coming to me. As a result, my team is usually able to work things out on their own. If they do come to me with a question or problem, I know they've already tried to come up with a solution, and now I'm really needed.

Conversely, I've found that a *lack* of cross-training can also contribute to culture problems. How can you help your coworkers if you don't actually know how to help them? Training everyone to be proficient in all areas of the business gives them the tools to help their coworkers and be a better team. That can go a long way toward improving a company's culture.

Cross-training is pretty simple; you just have to take the time to do it. We set aside time every quarter where we just shut down the office for a day and spend a portion of that time training and retraining. (The rest is reserved for a fun activity, which I'll talk about in a second.)

One day we might have the techs train our optical team on the basics of teching, another day we might have the front desk staff teach the rest of the team about the basics of working the front desk. Obviously, we're not going to be able to teach every little detail of every role to every person in our practice. That's not the point; the point is to give everyone enough knowledge to help with the basics if needed, and to open their eyes to what the rest of the team is doing and how the practice is working as a whole.

One thing I've found, which you might relate to, is that everyone always thinks they have the hardest job or that they're doing the most work. One employee might feel like they have a million things to do while the rest of the team is just sitting around doing nothing. But the reality is that everyone has a lot of work on their plate; you just don't always see it. When we do cross-training, I love to first have everyone go around and say one thing they do that the team probably doesn't realize they do. It's a great way to show the team that everyone is working hard and that their work matters.

Another benefit of cross-training is that your team may find better ways of working together. They might realize that a slight change to the way they work can help someone in another department. That's a win-win for everyone!

Fun Friday

At the end of every quarter, we have what's called Fun Friday, where we close the office and spend time training, retraining, and having fun. Since it's the end of the quarter, we can also look at the numbers and go over our bonus system to see how much money everyone is going to get based on our performance.

We spend the first part of the day cross-training, talking about our goals for the practice, and reviewing the metrics to understand where we're at. If things are going really well, this might be short. But we always have this time set aside to practice, to review the fundamentals, and to get together as a group to talk about the practice. One crucial point is that we work on what the team wants to work on. I'll often just open it up to the team and ask them what they want to work on—usually, they have a few things they've been wanting to learn or address or improve, so this is our time to do that. Remember, this isn't just about what you want. Always involve your team!

In the afternoon, we go do something fun as a group, and we still end at 4:00 pm so everyone gets to go home at a normal time. I don't want to intrude on anyone's family time. The last time we did this, we went to an escape room, which was a blast. Another one we've done a few times is a pottery class where they get to make their own pottery. Whatever it is, it's a great chance for everyone to let their hair down and have some fun together. It's great for team bonding, and it's a heck of a lot better than just spending all day training at the office.

Now, I really think the "fun" part is just as important as the training part. If we go back to our sports analogy, the best sports teams aren't just the ones that practice the most or have the best players. The best teams are the ones with great chemistry. They do things away from the field or the court—they have fun, they bond, and they build relationships with each other.

If you want proof of this, just look at the 2004 Boston Red Sox team that won the World Series and broke the curse of the Bambino. That team may not have been the best on paper, but boy, did they have chemistry. They all grew beards together, they joked around, they called themselves "the idiots," and they blasted music and danced in the clubhouse before every game. If you watched them play that year, you could tell that they just genuinely seemed to like each other. It was infectious. They went on to have one of the greatest comebacks in sports history and break an 86-year-old curse.

I firmly believe the same concept applies to business. Chemistry is what separates good teams from great ones, and you build it by letting loose and having fun together.

Your Team is the Foundation of Your Practice

If there's one thing I've learned, it's that you can have the best technology, the most beautiful office, and the most sophisticated marketing, but if you don't have the right people who genuinely care about your success and your patients' wellbeing, none of it matters.

It took a long time for me to learn this lesson. My journey didn't happen overnight, and yours won't either, but it can happen a lot sooner if you shift your thinking. The biggest take-away I'd like you to get from this chapter is that *you get from your team what you put into them.* Your staff is not an expense, they're an investment. And when you invest money, time, and energy into your team, you will get it back tenfold.

Remember: good people help you grow your practice. But more than that, good people make work enjoyable. They make you excited to walk through that back door every morning. They turn your practice from a place you *have* to be into a place you *want* to be.

But building a great team is only the first step. Once you have the right people in place and you've trained them effectively, you need to know how to lead them effectively. You need to create a culture where they want to work hard for you, even when you're not watching. You need systems to hold them accountable without crushing their morale, and you need to know how to make those tough decisions when someone isn't the right fit.

That's exactly what we're going to cover in the next chapter. I'm going to show you the leadership philosophy that transformed my practice from a place where people worked *for* me into a place where people work *with* me. You'll learn the "I, We, Y'all" approach that builds loyalty, how to create a family atmosphere that patients can feel the moment they walk through your door, and why being generous with your team is actually one of the smartest business decisions you can make.

We'll also tackle the hard stuff—like my zero-tolerance policy for negativity and how to implement a system of accountability that's fair, consistent, and actually helps your team members grow rather than just punishing them when they make mistakes.

But for now, just remember: your team is the foundation of your practice, and you get out of them what you put into them!

Key Takeaways

1. **Pay well and expect more.** When you invest in better people and pay them appropriately, they will generate far more revenue than the extra cost. If you average $400 per exam and hire someone at $20 an hour, if they can help you see just two more patients a day, that is $640 more gross revenue!

2. **Hire for attitude, train for skill.** The worst prerequisite for working in an optometry practice is experience in another optometry practice. Look for people who make others feel good, who stay positive under pressure, and who genuinely care about helping people. You can teach them the right skills, but you can't teach them to have a good heart.

3. **Trust your team by training your team.** Most performance problems are training problems in disguise. When someone isn't performing well, ask yourself: "Did I give them the tools and training they need to succeed?" Create systems for cross-training and delegate meaningful responsibilities. The goal is to delegate everything outside of the exam room.

3.
Leading Your Team

____

In the last chapter, we talked about how to build a great team by hiring the right people, paying them well, and setting them up for success through training. But having great people is only half the battle. The other half is learning how to lead them effectively.

Now, I'll start by saying something slightly controversial. A lot of people don't like to describe their team as a "family." I know some consultants and business experts will tell you that you shouldn't be friends with your staff, or that to be a good leader you need to maintain a professional distance between you and your team.

To that I would say: *what a shitty life that is.* (Pardon my French, but there's just no other way to put this.) I mean, you spend 40 hours a week for most of your life with these people. You really don't want to be friends with them? And I had no idea the French cussed so much.

Life is short. And what I realized, especially after those three guys passed away—my dad, my brother, and Dr. Foster—is that if you've got a really happy team and you treat them like family, and they know you've got their back and they've got yours, you will create an environment that patients will go out of their way for.

I'm not afraid to say that my team is my family. I take care of them, and they take care of me and our patients. Without my team, I'd be nothing. I will remove patients if they're rude to my team, no questions asked. If they have a sick kid at home, they don't have to ask me to stay home—they know they can take as much time as they need. I hug them every morning. (Okay, not like a full-on hug, it's more of a side hug and "good morning" kinda thing, but you get the idea.)

The thing is, I think most optometrists and business leaders in general would love to have a good relationship with their team, but they also want their team to perform well. It might seem like you have to pick one or the other, but you don't. You just have to follow this formula:

Generosity + Leadership = Performance

My dad taught me early on that "you can't outgive God," and that's something that has really shaped how I approach leadership. When you're generous with your team—not just financially, but when you genuinely invest in their wellbeing—it comes back to you in ways you never expected. And when I talk about generosity, I'm talking about *true* generosity. Not just giving someone more money, but being genuinely caring about the people you work with as human beings. Caring about their families, what's going on in their lives, their struggles, their wins, and yes—their income.

When Hurricane Helene went through Tennessee in 2024, one of my staff members lost her home. It was completely destroyed, and the whole situation was just a total nightmare for her. We own a rental house, so my wife and I decided she could live there rent-free for as long as she needed. She ended up staying there with her family for about four months while she dealt with insurance and figured out her next steps.

We didn't do that because it was a smart business decision, we did it because we genuinely care about her, and it was the right thing to do. We are glad we were able to help her.

The same goes for anyone on my team—they know that I will go out of my way to help them if they need it. If someone has a health issue that is going to prevent them from working for a while, for example, I'll give them extra paid time off so they don't use up all their vacation or sick time. The same goes for anyone having a baby.

I don't do these things to build loyalty, improve team morale, or boost company culture. Our bottom line is certainly not a factor. I do these things because I genuinely care about my team. They are my family, and I care for them like my family. And what do I get in return? My team would move mountains for our practice. They work hard, they care, they perform, and perhaps above all, they stay by my side. That doesn't just happen by being a good leader. It happens by being a generous leader.

Oh, and I absolutely love coming to work and hanging out with these people every day. It ROCKS!

Working "With" Your Team

The biggest mindset shift that most leaders need to have is that they are not above their team; they are part of the team. One simple way to make that shift is through your language, and your team will pick up on this right away. Case in point: I never say that somebody *works* for me; I say they work *with* me.

It might sound arbitrary, but it's amazing how the way you say things can affect the way people react. When I introduce someone at meetings now, I don't say, "This is Stephanie, she works for me." I say, "Stephanie and I work together. She's our optical manager, and we're a team."

Do you see the difference that makes? My team is not beneath me; they're with me. We're partners. We're in this together.

There's also a level of respect that comes with that type of language, and I want my team to both like and respect me. I've always worked on the philosophy that if people are working for you because they're afraid of you or because "you're the boss," they'll work hard when you're watching. If they like you and respect you, they will work hard for you when you're not watching. This is something I've certainly encountered in my coaching—there is a big difference in performance when you compare teams who actually want to work and those who are being forced to work.

When people are only working for you out of fear or because you're the boss, you become more of a "workplace police officer" than a leader. If you feel like you are constantly having to check on people to make sure they're doing their jobs, that might be a sign that you're leading through fear versus respect. Working like that is exhausting for you and demoralizing for your team.

When your team likes you and respects you, they'll work hard because they want to see you and the business succeed. They take ownership of their responsibilities and go above and beyond without being asked. They solve problems on their own instead of waiting for you to tell them what to do. I think I know which type of work environment you'd like to have.

The thing is, you can't fake this. If you're only being nice to your team because you think it will make them work harder, they'll see right through it. You have to *genuinely* care, and it has to show up consistently in your actions. One of the best ways to do that? Lead by example! Show your team that you will do anything you ask them to do, and that you're ready to get in the trenches with them if need be.

Leading by Example

If you're not willing to do a job yourself, why should you expect your team to do it? One trait of great leaders is that they're willing to do anything they ask of their team, whether that's getting a patient ready yourself when all the techs are busy or cleaning the dishes in the break room. This type of leadership does two things: It shows your team that their work is not beneath you, and they know that you'll be able to help them if they're ever in a pinch.

In Chapter 2, I went on and on about how practically everything outside of the eye exam itself should be delegated. That is absolutely the goal, but even if you're a master delegator, you will sometimes be put in situations where you need to handle things that are outside of your normal routine.

For example, I will tech my own patients when we need it. Three of our employees have had babies within the last eight months, and they were all techs. So, some days we had one tech and other days we had none. I just went up there and started teching my own patients. I didn't make them feel guilty or tell them they needed to get back to work as soon as possible because I couldn't stand doing their job. I just got it done.

Just last week, I came into the break room and one of my employees was bawling her eyes out. She had just found out her mother-in-law was really sick, and it wasn't looking good. I hugged her, I asked her what was going on, and I told her to take the day off. She said, "But I can't leave, I'm your only tech today."

I looked at her and said, "I can tech. Go. Now. If something happens to her, you're going to regret not being there way more than you're going to regret leaving work early. I'm pulling the boss card—you're going to see your mother-in-law."

My office manager told me later that moment really meant a lot to this person. And her mother-in-law did recover, thankfully. But if she hadn't, she would have been there in those final moments because we made sure work didn't get in the way of what really mattered.

Leading by example also means honoring your commitments. My grandfather's middle name was Thomas, and I was named after him. That's why I always sign my name "Kurt T. Steele"—the T is a reminder of my grandfather, and he once taught me a valuable lesson in leadership.

My granddad was big on follow-through. His philosophy was: If you say you're going to do something, do it. Always. No excuses. Your word is your bond.

When he passed away, his funeral happened to land on a day I had committed to speaking at an event in Miami, and the date had been on my calendar for months. I was torn. Of course, I wanted to be at the funeral to honor him. But I'd also made a commitment to those people in Miami.

I went to the funeral. And then immediately afterward, I got on a plane and flew to Miami to keep my speaking commitment. Looking back, I know that's exactly what my granddad would have told me to do. In fact, I like to think I did it because of him. He would have said, "You told those people in Miami you were going to speak. You need to honor that commitment."

Your team is watching whether you do what you say you're going to do. If you commit to something and don't follow through, they notice. If you make promises you don't keep, they lose trust in you. But if you consistently honor your commitments—even when it's hard, even when it's inconvenient—they learn that your word means something. And by the way, *the same goes for your patients.*

When your team knows that you have their back, they'll move mountains for you. And one of the best ways to do that is to lead by example. There is no work in your practice that is beneath you. You should be ready and willing to jump in wherever you're needed, because that's what a good team member does. And you are a part of the team.

Setting the Culture

Not many people can say they remember the dumbest thing they've ever said, but I can. I'm not sure if that's something to be proud of, but I'll share it with you anyway because it was a big lesson I had to learn the hard way.

A few years ago, my optical manager came up to me and said, "You know, we skipped Fun Friday this last quarter, and you can actually tell that morale is down just a little."

My response was, "Well, there are 15 of you and there are two of us, so you really have more control over morale than we do."

That is by far the dumbest thing I've ever said as a business owner. I basically told my team that the morale in our office isn't my responsibility, which is just wrong on so many levels. I was avoiding the responsibility of being a leader and putting the blame on my team for something that was clearly not their fault.

A team's culture starts with its leader. Period. If you're having culture problems with your team, you need to start by looking at yourself and your leadership style. Your attitude and the way you behave have more effect on your team's culture than anything else. You set the standard, and you permit what type of behavior is or isn't allowed. Remember, you are part of the team—so if there's a culture problem, that means you're part of it.

My wife used to be a sales rep, and she would tell me stories that proved this time and time again. She'd visit a practice where a great person worked, and when that person left to go work for a "not-so-nice" office, they would immediately take on the attitude of that new practice. On the flip side, when someone who was maybe not so great would leave a bad office and start at a practice with great culture, that person would often transform into a star performer.

The leader sets the tone, and everyone else follows. That's not always easy, either—it can be really hard. I've had mornings where I'm sitting in my truck, almost crying, and wondering how I'm going to get through the day. But when I walk through that back door, you better believe I'm putting on a smile for my team, no matter what's happening in my life. You've got to be the ray of sunshine every single day, because your attitude will be the attitude of your staff.

Do I slip occasionally?" Of course I do. And I always regret it, but I'm also always quick to apologize for it. I can never remember one time in 30 years being critical of my staff—especially in front of patients—and not regretting it.

"I, We, Y'all" Leadership

If you were to take one technique away from this chapter, this would be it. The "I, We, Y'all" Leadership Philosophy is something I've used for years, and it came from an unlikely source. If you haven't caught on by now, I am a huge Tennessee Volunteers

(Vols) football fan. I've been going to Tennessee games for as long as I can remember, and I have a cousin I can proudly say played for them (Doug Baird). While my good friend, coach Phillip Fulmer, was there, we went 11-5 against Alabama. But he had a hard time with Coach Nick Saban, as most everybody else did. It's hard to argue the fact that he was the greatest college football coach of all time. It's probably not even up for debate.

Whenever Alabama lost a game—which wasn't very often—Saban would take responsibility. He never threw his team under the bus. He'd come out to the press conference and say something like, "I didn't have them ready to play today, this one's on me." I never once saw him blame anyone besides himself, even when it was obviously the fault of one player in particular.

My dad used to coach high school basketball in the 70s, and he did the same thing. He had high expectations for his team, and he took their games seriously, but one thing I never saw him do was yell at a player during a game. Why? Because, in his words, "If they're not ready to play the game, that's not their fault. That's my fault." It was his job as the coach to prepare them, so if they weren't performing well, it was because he didn't do his job right.

Now, that didn't mean he went easy on them in practice! It was the opposite, really. He was tough on them in practice, but during games, he was calm and treated his players with respect.

For us, training is our practice, and seeing patients is the game. The same principle applies.

That philosophy is the mark of a great leader, and it's the first part of the "I, We, Y'all" Leadership Philosophy. Here's how it works.

When something goes wrong, I take the blame: "I'm sorry, **I** really screwed this up."

When there's a problem that needs to be solved, we solve it together: "Okay team, how are **we** going to fix this?"

And when the problem is solved, they get the credit: "Wow, **y'all** did a great job fixing this."

As a leader, you will be faced with problems in your business. How you respond to them will dictate how you come out on the other side. Good leaders take the blame, get input from their team, and give out praise. Great leaders will do all of that even when the problem had nothing to do with them.

Whenever we have a problem in our business or I want to make a change, I start by blaming myself. I'll go to my team and say, "Y'all, I really screwed this up. This is going on, and I made a mistake. How do you think we should fix this?" And then I shut up. I let them tell me what they think we should do because nine times out of ten, they will know more about how to solve the problem than I do. They are the ones that are doing the majority of "work" in our business, so they not only deserve a say in how we operate, but they should be taking the lead.

Usually, they give me a great idea. And when they fix it, even if I did a lot of the work, I say, "Boy, y'all fixed this. Y'all did a great job. Thank you so much."

I'm pretty sure if every optometrist followed this strategy, I'd practically be out of a job as a coach. I mean, seriously, it just makes everything better. When you include your team in solving the problem, they take ownership and are more likely to solve the problem successfully. I can think of plenty of times where I let my team take the lead on solving a problem, and they found a better solution than I could have. Or they've even come to me and said, "Hey, we fixed that and also came up with this new idea that will save us time," or save the company money. That's what happens when you actively collaborate with your team instead of ordering them around.

So next time you encounter a problem in your business, just remember: "I, We, Y'all." (I suppose you can change it to "you all" if you're not from the South…)

Removing Friction Points

Team culture always starts with the leader, and up to this point, we've covered a lot of methods you can use to improve yourself as a leader and develop a winning culture. But at the end of the day, the leader can only do so much, and unfortunately, there will be times when you need to make tough decisions. When there is friction among your team, it needs to be dealt with. If the problem persists, it might mean someone needs to be let go.

Many of the optometrists I've coached struggle with firing people. Specifically, they struggle with knowing when to make the call to let someone go and how to do it. I get it. No one wants to be the bad guy! I've spoken at length about how you should be friends with your team, and dealing out punishments or firing people runs directly counter to that. For that reason, I've had the same nervousness and anxiety around firing people that you've probably had. But all that went away when I developed a *system* for it.

If someone in our practice gets let go, it is not because I chose to fire them on a whim; it is because of the System of Accountability we have in place. My whole team knows how this system works and has agreed to it. It's fair and equal—everyone plays by the same rules. The brilliance of this system is that it lets me hold people accountable for their actions in a way that doesn't ruin my relationship with them or alienate me from the rest of my team. If you're going to be a nice boss, you can't be a pushover either. This system is a great way to find a balance between the two.

The System of Accountability

I originally learned about this system from a book called *Discipline Without Punishment* by Dick Grote, although I've since added my own spin on this. That's a common theme you're going to see the more you get to know me, by the way. I don't just think of this stuff out of thin air; I borrow ideas from people, and I often tweak things to make them work well for me and my practice. Case in point: I don't love the word punishment, which is why I call this the System of Accountability, since that's really what it is meant to do—hold people accountable.

My version of this system breaks everything down into three categories: attendance, conduct, and performance. If someone's actions aren't aligning with your expectations for those three areas, this system can hold them accountable and provide a way for them to get back on track.

By the way, did you notice how there's no "attitude" there? That's because you can't change someone's attitude. If there's an attitude problem, that might be a sign to skip this system altogether and let them go immediately. More on that later.

What you can expect, however, is professional conduct. One of my favorite things to say to my team is, "You don't have to like working here, you just have to act like it." I can't make your attitude change, but if you're going to work here, you need to be professional with our patients and coworkers.

The System of Accountability has four steps. If you're experiencing a problem with one of your employees, you can simply start with step one. If that doesn't solve the problem, move on to step two, and so on. If all four steps have been completed and there is still no change in behavior, then you've done everything you can and that person should likely be terminated.

Let's take a look at how this all works.

Step 1: Clarification & Support Session

In Chapter 2, I mentioned how most employee problems are more like training problems. That's why the first step of The System of Accountability is to offer clarification and support. The purpose here is to ensure the employee fully understands the expectations within their role, identify any barriers to performance, and offer immediate support as needed. This is a collaborative, non-punitive conversation.

Recommended Action: Meet with your employee one-on-one to clearly define the expectation, discuss the observed gap, and ask, "What support do you need to meet this?" or "What's getting in the way?" Be sure to document the conversation along with any agreed-upon support and a timeline for improvement.

Step 2: Formal Goal Setting

If there is no positive change after the initial clarification and support session, the next step is to conduct a more formal goal-setting session. This is for more persistent, significant performance gaps. It formalizes the process and sets specific, measurable goals with consequences if they are not met. While the first step is more about support and encouragement, this next step is about accountability. You're letting the employee know that you've held up your end of the bargain, and you need them to hold up theirs.

Recommended Action: Hold a documented meeting to review the lack of improvement from step one. Set specific, measurable, achievable, relevant, time-bound (SMART) goals in line with your expectations for the role. Initiate a formal performance improvement plan (PIP) outlining expectations, resources, and a reminder of the system in place for non-compliance. If all goals are met, this can be cleaned off the employee's record within three months of no further incidents.

Step 3: Corrective Action

If the goals from step two aren't achieved within the specified timeframe, there needs to be corrective action. This is the second formal step, and frankly, it's where things get a lot more serious. At this point, you have given the employee everything they need to succeed and they are still not complying with your requests.

Recommended Action: Issue a written warning detailing the specific performance deficiencies, referencing prior discussions and the PIP. Reiterate expectations, consequences of continued non-performance, and specify a final period for improvement. If all goals are met, this can also be cleaned off the employee's record with six months of no further incidents.

Step 4: Final Decision & Action

It's time to make a final decision. If performance expectations are still not met at this point, there needs to be consequences. You can think of this as the last strike—they have no more chances after this.

Recommended Action: Give the employee a day off with pay to decide whether they would like to continue working at your company. If any further incidents occur within a year, the position is officially terminated.

The System in Action

Let me give you an example of how this can work in practice. I had an employee once who was chronically late. You know the type—always showing up eight to ten minutes late, which might not seem like a big deal, but when it happens consistently, it becomes a real problem. It isn't fair to everyone else who makes it on time. We went through the system with her, and we got to step three.

At step three, I had a serious conversation with her, and all I had to do was remind her of the system (which she was well aware of). I told her:

"Look, I love having you as an employee, but this attendance problem cannot continue. This is the system we have in place, and you're at step three. The next time you're late, you might as well stay home, because that's your decision-making day. And if you're late again after that, according to the system we have in place, you won't have a job here anymore."

I know this might sound harsh, but the reality is that we're running a business and we have to hold ourselves to certain standards. I can sympathize with them as a friend, but as the owner of our business, I need to be firm. Sometimes I'll even say that outright:

"Listen, your friend Kurt sympathizes with you, and I'm sorry that's the situation you're in. But Dr. Steele, who runs this office, has to keep this business running. We have patients scheduled at specific times, we have hours we're open, and we have a system in place. This is the system, and this is where we're at."

Wouldn't you know it, she wasn't late again for years. I didn't have to yell at her, I didn't have to argue, and our relationship stayed intact. I also didn't have to wonder if I was doing the right thing, agonizing over a tough decision—all I had to do was follow the system we've agreed to.

The beauty of this system is that it removes emotion from the equation and ensures consistency. It also covers you as the employer in a legal sense. I have ended up on the phone with an unemployment judge twice, and the first question they always ask is, "Was the employee aware this was a problem?" I told them, "Well, yes. We coached them, we implemented a performance improvement plan, we gave them a written warning, and we had a decision-making leave where we let them go home for a day with pay to think about it. So, they had four opportunities to improve, and they did not. And we have all of that documented."

In both cases, the judge apologized for wasting my time and told me to be on my way.

You Set the Tone

Before we close out this chapter, there's one thing I want to make abundantly clear. *That which is tolerated is accepted.* And what I mean by that is that you permit the behavior of your team based on what you tolerate. You set the tone. If you will tolerate any type of behavior, then your team is going to behave however they want. If you have specific things that you will not tolerate—and your team is aware of those—then they will act accordingly.

The System of Accountability is great for most problems you'll encounter in the workplace. In rare cases, however, you might need to escalate things, and it's up to you to decide what that threshold is. At the end of the day, you *do* have the power to let anyone go for any reason. It's your business and you get to decide what is acceptable or not!

For example, there are two things that I simply will not tolerate in my business, and those are negativity and theft. My team knows that they can be let go immediately for either one. In fact, it's something I tell everyone during the hiring process, so they're clear on it from day one.

Theft should be pretty obvious. To me, that is just a no-brainer. I am not going to let someone steal from our business and get away with it—end of story.

The negativity one is something that came to me after those three guys passed away. Life is just too short to come to work every day and deal with a negative attitude—that's just something I won't put up with. And remember, you can't change attitude. I will give them a chance to improve their conduct, but attitude is something I have very little control over.

I can also say from my own experience and from the optometrists I've coached that a negative person will kill your practice. I have a hunch that you know this from experience.

Most of us have had that employee whom we knew we should let go, and for one reason or another, we kept them for way too long. Every single time that's happened in my business, when I finally let them go, I've had people coming to me and saying, "Oh, thank you so much. Thank you for getting rid of that person."

When those three guys passed away, we parted ways with three people within six months because they were so negative. My team not only thanked me, they told me that their lives were made easier by *removing* those people. Even though they had to take on more work as a result, the removal of that friction made their job easier and more enjoyable.

And by the way, this same philosophy applies to your patients, too. You also permit their behavior, and you have the power to remove patients if they're problematic. This is a great way to show your team that you have their back.

Just a couple of weeks ago, I had a guy drop an f-bomb on my optician. The next day, he got a letter from me telling him he was no longer welcome in our practice. I know some practice owners might hesitate to fire a patient because they're worried about lost revenue. But this is serious stuff. When you allow patients to abuse your team, you're telling your employees that keeping that patient's money is more important than their dignity and well-being. That's not the message I want to send.

Besides, patients who are rude to your staff are usually not the patients you want anyway. They're often the ones who complain the most, pay the least, and create the most problems. When you remove those patients from your practice, you're actually improving the overall patient experience for everyone else.

Your team spends their days taking care of people, often dealing with insurance hassles, scheduling conflicts, and all sorts of patient concerns. The least you can do is make sure they don't have to deal with abuse on top of everything else.

Retention & Development

It should be clear by now that if you hire good people and treat them well, you will avoid 90% of personnel problems in the workplace. But avoiding problems is just scratching the surface of what a great team can do for your practice. You will also create such a fun, awesome place to work that patients will love coming to your office. And perhaps most importantly, you will start to retain long-term employees who can grow with your practice.

You've heard me talk about how long my team members have been with me, but it wasn't always like that. When I first started my practice, I dealt with lots of turnover. It was awful! It was a headache for me, and it had a big effect on our patient experience. Seeing new faces every year at your eye exam isn't exactly comforting. You have to wonder what's going on behind the scenes…

The turning point was when I made a conscious decision to put my team first. That's when people started staying longer, and when that happened, I was also able to develop some of them into leaders. This is something that every good leader should be striving toward, but it's just not possible if you're dealing with constant turnover.

One of my favorite examples is Molly, our current office manager. She started working with us when she was 18 years old. Now, I will tell you that Molly is just a very even-keeled person. She's smart, she has a great head on her shoulders, and she is just very consistent with everything she does—she's a great coworker. So five years into her time with us, she was 23 years old and working part-time while she went to college.

She was actually about to graduate when she came to me one day and said, "Dr. Steele, I really want to talk to you." And let's just say it was not in the tone of "I am so happy!" I could tell something was off, so we went to Waffle House—because they can't slap you in a Waffle House… I don't think.

We sat down, and she started to tell me that she found out she was making a dollar per hour less than another employee of mine. She said, "Dr. Steele, I've been here two years longer than they have, I trained them, and they're awesome. But I can do more than they can, and my feelings are hurt that they're making more than I am. I just want an explanation." It wasn't negative, it was very professional. I was really impressed with the way she handled this.

So I looked at Molly, and I said, "Molly, I agree with everything you just said, but there's a part of the pay scale that you're not thinking of, and that is called retention. You're getting your master's in counseling in May, and you've already informed us you're leaving to go be a counselor, so we're not trying to retain you. And by the way, you're doing such a great job that, if it'll make you feel better, I will bump your pay up another dollar over the next four months. You're that much a part of our family. But the thing is, I don't really have an incentive to raise your pay more because we're losing you."

She looked at me and said, "Wow, that did not occur to me. And that is perfectly fair." She went back to eating, and that was basically the end of the conversation.

I remember thinking how she handled the whole situation just perfectly—she was professional, respectful, kind, everything you want in a great employee. I thought *that should be the way I should be able to talk to my office manager,* which I could not do with my current office manager at the time. So, I looked up what a counselor makes in the state of Tennessee. I was paying my current office manager more than that, and it occurred to me that I could pay Molly more than she would make as a counselor and retain her in a higher role.

I ended up promoting Molly to office manager, and she's been with us ever since. The best part is that right after I did that, I had multiple employees come to me and tell me that it was a great decision. Even Amie, who had been with us the longest, came to me and said, "That will be one of the best moves you ever make." That's because they worked with Molly, and they knew how great a team member she was. They also wanted what was best for our practice, and making Molly our office manager was the best thing for everyone. It didn't matter that she was 23 years old and didn't have experience as an office manager—we all knew she was the right person for the job. Looking back, I actually think that is one of the smartest business decisions I've ever made.

Peyton Manning is one of the greatest quarterbacks of all time and should have won the Heisman in 1997. He went on to win two Super Bowls, and he's still synonymous with Tennessee football. However, Tennessee won their National Championship after Peyton Manning left them, along with three other first-round draft picks and 12 players who played in the NFL. That was because Tee Martin was the quarterback, and the team really respected him. They had a chip on their shoulder and wanted to prove that he was a great leader. They wanted to win for him.

We've also talked about team chemistry, and the defense had a leader named Al Wilson that everyone followed. One of my best friends in this world is Coach John Chavis, and he is one of the best defensive coordinators in the history of football, in my opinion. He told me that this team was easy to coach because he didn't have to coach effort. Al Wilson made sure that everybody hustled all the time. The key lesson here is you need both a quarterback (office manager) that everybody admires, respects, and wants to work hard for—but you also need a team leader that makes sure everybody's hustling and doing their job.

That decision also showed my team that we invest in people and that there are opportunities to advance in our practice. And really, it's just one of many examples of times where we've made the conscious decision to invest in our people. In later chapters, we'll even cover the bonus system we use that shows how we financially invest in our team and show our appreciation for them every quarter.

When you invest in your people, they invest in you. It's that simple.

Your Team Comes First

In the next chapter, we'll cover metrics. People have told me for years that I explain metrics in a different way than most, and that I make them very easy and practical. Really, I just think a lot of people overcomplicate this stuff. As you'll see, metrics don't need to be complicated and just understanding the basics will get you far.

But as useful as metrics are, they aren't going to do much good if you are having problems with your team. If you're dealing with subpar performance or having to hire new techs every few months because people are constantly quitting, metrics aren't going to move the needle for you. Your team is the foundation that makes everything else in your practice more impactful. That's why we covered it first. Everything else will build on that foundation.

And remember, part of the goal of this book is to help you build a practice you love. A great team will make your company a great place to work. Just to give you an idea of what this can look like, I sent the following text to my team and every single person responded within 20 minutes.

Here was the text: "Hey guys, I am hearing lots of doctors talk about having problems with their staff, and we don't have that problem. Why do we have such a good place to work?"

Here are their responses:

- "I would say there's a culture that's been fostered where we always know you will put us and our families first. Therefore, if we take care of you, you will take care of us. I think that culture was built way before I came here by you and Jeff."

- "You guys care about family. You guys let us put our kids first, and when something happens in our lives, y'all have our backs and are there for us. The workplace is more like a family than just coworkers."

- "Good people attract more good people. If your current team is happy, they likely tell others. And those referrals are gold—they come in already trusting the environment."

- "I believe the reason we have such a good team is that we have a good manager. Molly and I work well as a team and can run ideas off each other when it comes to the rest of the team."

- "The team is always focusing on their strengths. Everyone has their own weaknesses, and too many people focus on those. When we focus on each individual's strengths instead of what they do wrong, it makes the atmosphere more positive. This helps everyone work better as a team when they hear what they're doing right!"

- "We're careful who we hire, and if they're not a good fit, we let them go. Molly does a great job weeding out people before we bring them in for the interview process, which helps tremendously. You and Emily are great bosses to work for, which is most important."

- "I think we do so well because we're appreciated."

- "We've gone through a couple of bad ones, but we find the right fits. We find people who want a work family. We work together because we've found people who want to please and love helping people, including each other.

We all generally enjoy each other. We have a Molly. Office manager is the key! I should have said that first."

- "It's hard to find what we have. But it all starts with who is in charge. We all know the docs are the boss, but the office manager is most definitely the key. They're the glue. Someone has to listen to your concerns and make you feel valued. Life is hard in general. Employees need to feel like they matter, and we most definitely have that. It's easy to work for a boss like that."

- "A very competitive pay rate, wonderful PTO, and most importantly, cross-trained staff that truly care about each other. We're always willing to step in and fill in wherever needed for our patients' best interest because we truly believe we're family, and that's what family does."

- "I think it's because of you guys, honestly. The freedom to be a mom first. And for us to be able to put family first. It's hard to find a job that will allow that. Most of our employees are moms that do have to run for our kids—doctors' appointments, sports, school events. And never once have y'all complained or fussed about it. So thank you! Also, you guys are really great about asking our opinions on a lot of things, such as hours and lunches. We get a voice in what goes on."

- "Hi! I really feel like it all boils down to the family-like environment that we create. Everyone helps each other out and never turns a blind eye. The training I received when I was hired was top-notch, and I feel like we love to see each other succeed in everything we do, not just at work. By far my favorite people I have ever worked with!"

- "Hi Dr. Steele, I think there are several reasons. One would be the culture that has been created. Everyone really is like family. We all help each other out willingly. Second, everyone seems to be cross-trained pretty well, so there's none of this 'it's not my job.' It's all of our job. Our focus is to help the patient with their needs and help make the doctors' jobs go smoothly. We all try to treat the patients like they're our neighbors. A smile and a greeting go a long way."

- "I think we're doing so well because we all seem to work well together and help each other. If one is out, we all come together to share the load. All the doctors are very understanding and good to work for, and the team is like family."

- "My first questions for the doctors having trouble finding good people would be: How do they treat them?

Do they make them feel like an 'employee,' just someone to do a job? Do they treat them like they are beneath them, only to speak to them when they need something? Then, they absolutely need to hear from Dr. Steele! I am proud to say our doctors are family! Y'all laugh, be silly, 'monkey on a cupcake.' You always ask how we are. Anything we can do to make it better? Tell us you appreciate us. I think of you as a brother! Like I said before, we are not employees, we are family! It's a great day to have a great day!"

Start with your team, and the rest will follow. I promise.

Key Takeaways

1. **Your team *should* be family.** You spend 40–50 (well, in my case 30–40) hours a week together. That's more time than many people spend with their actual family! Why wouldn't you want to be close with your team? When you treat them like family, they'll work with you, not just for you. Genuinely caring for your team will create an environment where they are motivated to do great work. I've said it before and I'll say it again: When you have their back, they'll have yours.

2. **Your team works with you, not for you.** The simple shift from saying that people work "with you" instead of "for you" can change the entire dynamic of your team. It shows your team that you've got their back. I don't even call my team employees; they are my coworkers! This language matters more than you think.

3. **Remember: "I, We, Y'all."** Take the blame when things go wrong, create solutions together, and give your team all the credit when things go right. This is one of the most important frameworks in this book, as it will help build trust and loyalty while also empowering your team to solve problems on their own. Your team often knows more about the problem than you do anyway! So you should absolutely include them in the solution.

My amazing Vision Source team!

Me, Dr. Foster, and my current practice partner,
Dr. Emily Eisenhower.

Dr. Foster and Amie, one of our longest-serving team members!

Part 2
The Metrics

4.
Performance Metrics

———————

When my dad was a high school basketball coach back in the 1970s, after every single game, he would grade each player's performance.

He had a whole system worked out. You got points for rebounds, points for scoring, and points for defensive hustle plays. He tracked everything on this clipboard he carried around. It sounds crazy, but he actually had a very good reason for doing this. He would use each person's grade to determine who played in the next game (and for how long). The top four or five grades? Those were your starters. If you got an F, you were going to be on the bench.

Now, this probably wouldn't be allowed today, but my dad actually gave you a negative point if you played more than half the game and didn't foul somebody. His thinking was that if you didn't foul anyone, you weren't playing hard enough. You were avoiding contact, and in his eyes, that meant you weren't really competing.

Keep in mind, this was the 1970s. Nowadays, we have endless analytics in sports. I am a sports fan myself, but I honestly couldn't tell you the difference between OBP and OPS or how slugging percentage is calculated in baseball. It's gotten pretty out there, but that was not the case in the 70s.

Looking back, it's pretty impressive what my dad was able to accomplish with his clipboard. I can guarantee you none of the other coaches in his leagues were tracking stats like he was, or even tracking them at all. Yet he did it, and he put that data to good use. He wasn't guessing about who should start. He knew exactly who was producing and who wasn't—it was all on his clipboard. The best part is that it quite literally paid off. My dad is still the only person who has ever led our school to the state tournament. He really was a great coach.

At the time, I didn't realize the significance of what my dad was doing. But over time, and especially as I started to grow my business, I started to understand the real value of what he had on that clipboard. *Metrics are not just numbers on a spreadsheet; they are decision-making tools.*

In life and business, you will be faced with many tough decisions. Too many people make decisions based on their instincts alone, just hoping everything will work out. Or they don't make a decision at all out of fear of failure. When it comes to growing your business, there is no replacement for hard data. Metrics are the tools that will not only help you make the right decisions in your business but give you the courage to make big changes.

Do You **Really** Know Your Practice?

How do you know if you're actually growing your practice? It might sound like a silly question, and you may be thinking, "Of course I know whether I'm growing or not!" But do you really? Do you have the data to back it up? Can you say how much you're growing by every quarter or every year? What if it's not as much as you think? Or what if you're actually declining?

Most optometrists I meet have a general sense of whether business is good or bad. They know when they're busy, they know when they're slow, and they definitely know when the bank account looks healthy. But for the most part, that's all they're relying on. Most optometrists are more or less flying blind (no pun intended), making decisions based on what they *think* or *feel* rather than what they *know*. That's a problem. You have to run your business by the numbers. If you are not using numbers, you are running on emotions and gut feelings—and that is not a recipe for success.

Even if things seem to be going well, you'll never really know what's going on under the surface until you start tracking metrics. Sometimes, outward success might be masking internal problems. Just as an example, one thing that drives me absolutely crazy is doctors who brag about being booked out months in advance. What is so great about that? Your patients waiting months to see you or the gold mine you're sitting on? That's a great example of something that might sound good on the surface, but when you dig into the details, you realize it's actually masking a problem.

Similarly, seeing lots of patients would appear to be good. But how much revenue are you generating per exam? If you're seeing lots of patients but generating very little revenue per exam, then you might actually be better off seeing *fewer* patients so you can spend more time with each patient. These are just a couple of examples that show why tracking metrics is important.

When I first started my practice, I didn't know any of this stuff. There's a saying that "most optometry practices are one month away from bankruptcy"—they just run by the seat of their pants, pay the bills, and take what's left. My practice was one of those, except sometimes there wasn't anything left over! In the first three years, our income was below average and sporadic. Some months we could pay ourselves a decent chunk of change, and some months we could barely pay the bills. I would go months at a time without taking a paycheck for myself.

Finally, I decided something had to change. I didn't know what my future held, but I knew I wasn't going to go on like this, not paying myself three out of 12 months. I realized we needed to have some sort of rudder to keep us on track. A budget would be a good place to start, since at the time we were just seeing patients and hoping it would all work out. So, I started reading books about metrics. I learned the basics, things like how many patients you should see per day, how much you should generate on average, and what an optometric budget should look like.

Once I learned those basics, I just took out a piece of paper and wrote down where we were at. I compared that to national norms, and I started to figure out where we were most deficient. That sheet of paper became what I call my "goal sheet," and I've been updating it ever since. I actually still have the original piece of paper pinned to the wall in my office. (Now it's all done on spreadsheets.)

I can look over at that paper right now and read that our cost of goods sold was 36% the first time I measured it, compared to the national norm of around 25–30%. I remember when I figured that out, the solutions just became so obvious. I went over to my practice partner, Dr. Foster, and told him, "Look, we need to get this cost of goods sold down. So we need to either buy fewer frames, negotiate better deals with our vendors, or go up on price a tad. I don't really care what we do, but we need to do something to get this down to a normal level."

There's an old saying from Peter Drucker, a famous management consultant, which I must have read in one of those books because it stayed with me: "What gets measured, gets managed." I believe that is true, and that little goal sheet proves it. When I started measuring our metrics, it changed the entire trajectory of my practice. I could finally start making decisions based on data. I could be confident I was making the right choices. I was able to set goals and tell you whether we were on track to hit them or not. I was finally *managing* our growth!

And you know what happened? Within a year, I had not only hit every goal on that piece of paper, but I had exceeded most of them. Ever since, I have run my practice almost entirely based on metrics. I remember one day when we were having a team meeting, and someone on our team even said to me, "Why are you always making decisions based on numbers?"

My senior practice partner looked over at me, then back at them, and replied, "What else are we supposed to look at?!"

I know a lot of people hate looking at spreadsheets and dealing with numbers. I get that, but one thing that might shift your mindset is to start thinking about metrics for what they are. Metrics aren't just numbers; they are tools that you can use to make the right decisions with confidence rather than guessing and hoping things work out. I don't know about you, but that sounds a whole lot more appealing to me.

Performance vs. Expense Metrics

Now, before we get into specific metrics, let's take a step back. I like to break business metrics down into two broad categories: performance metrics and expense metrics.

Performance metrics tell you how well you're doing. For us, that means things like how much revenue you're generating per exam, how many patients you're seeing, and how well you're capturing opportunities with each patient. These are the numbers that show whether you're growing and how efficiently you're operating.

Expense metrics tell you how well you're managing your costs. So that will include things like how much you're paying your staff, cost of goods sold, overhead, and so on. These numbers show whether you're spending money wisely and maintaining healthy profit margins.

Both categories are essential. You can have great performance metrics, but if your spending is out of control, it won't do you much good. In the same vein, you could be great at controlling costs but missing opportunities because you're not investing in the right areas. This is actually quite common—everyone wants to save money, but the old lesson that "you need to spend money to make money" does still apply.

The key is finding a balance between the two. In this chapter, we'll focus on performance metrics. This is a great place to start because you need to first understand your baseline level of performance. Once you understand that, you'll be much better equipped to make decisions about your expenses.

That's why we're going to focus on performance metrics in this chapter, and then tackle expense metrics in the next one.

The Performance Metrics You Need to Know

I'm going to be referring to a lot of different metrics in the following pages, so I've included a list of the most helpful metrics to track and their definitions here. Keep in mind, these are *my* definitions. You might get a slightly different (and probably more "academic") definition if you do your own research. I prefer to keep things simple.

You may want to throw a bookmark in this page to refer back to these definitions as you read, or if you'd like, you can also download the PDF version at www.DrKurtSteele.com.

PERFORMANCE METRIC DEFINITIONS

Revenue: The total amount of money you deposit into the bank. Not what is in your electronic health record (EHR), but what is in QuickBooks—or whatever accounting software you use.

Revenue per doctor: The total revenue generated by each doctor. This is more than just your total revenue divided by the number of doctors. In my practice, I use the EHR report to come up with each doctor's percentage of collections, then I apply those percentages to our total revenue. For example, if we deposited $200,000 in QuickBooks in a month, and our EHR says I was responsible for 28% of collections, I am responsible for $56,000 in revenue.

Number of exams: I count this as any comprehensive annual exam (what a lot of people call an annual exam)—when I haven't seen someone in a year and they are receiving all tests.

Number of patients: Total number of patients seen (regardless of reason).

Revenue per exam: Revenue divided by number of exams.

Revenue per patient: Revenue divided by number of patients.

Revenue per day: Revenue divided by number of days worked. Critically, each doctor will have their own revenue per day metric. One way to think about this is "revenue per doctor day," but for the sake of brevity, I'll just refer to this as revenue per day.

Revenue per hour: Revenue per day divided by eight hours (or whatever is considered a full day in your practice). To track this, you'll need to make sure you're logging days worked, which may include decimals. (If you work a half day, log it as 0.5.)

Exam percentage: Number of exams divided by number of patients.

Cash flow: Whatever's left after paying everyone, including the partners.

New patient counts: People who haven't been in your office before or haven't been in for three years.

Total patient volume: This is everybody who walks through your door, no matter why they're there.

Patient retention rates: This tells you how many of your patients actually come back.

New vs. established patient percentages: This is the breakdown of how many new patients you see compared to established ones.

> ### OPTICAL-SPECIFIC METRICS
>
> *These metrics dive deeper into what you're selling and are the*
> *main drivers behind your revenue per exam.*
>
> **Capture Rate:** The percentage of glasses you sell compared to comprehensive exams.
>
> **Annual supply of contacts:** The percentage of patients who purchase an annual supply of contacts versus monthly or quarterly.
>
> **Dailies vs. monthlies:** The percentage of patients who wear daily lenses versus monthly lenses.
>
> **Transitions:** The percentage of glasses-wearers who purchase Transitions® lenses.
>
> **Second pairs of glasses:** The percentage of glasses-wearers who purchase one or more additional pairs of glasses.

"It Depends"

"What's the fastest way to increase revenue?" I get this question all the time. It's probably the one question that every business owner wants to know the answer to. Now, back when Dr. Foster and I were seeing one patient an hour, my simple answer used to be that the more people you can see, the more money you're going to make. The more I grew my practice, the more I learned that's not always the case. Really, it's a little more complicated.

Nowadays, I give the same answer every time, and you're probably not going to like it: "It depends."

The fastest way to grow revenue depends entirely on where you're at in your practice and what your current metrics are showing you. There is not going to be one clear answer that will apply to everyone. Generally speaking, however, there are two big levers you can use to increase revenue: **increase your number of exams** or **increase your revenue per exam.** These are, by and large, what you should be looking at if you want to increase your revenue. But there is a bell curve here, and which one you should focus on will depend on where you currently sit on that curve.

Obviously, you can increase your number of exams by improving your efficiency so you can get patients in and out quicker. If you're not currently booked up, you could also increase that number through marketing techniques or other strategies to bring more patients in the door.

Increasing revenue per exam is a little more nuanced, but it's one that I find many doctors don't spend enough time on. For the most part, you can increase revenue per exam by spending more time with patients and working on how you speak to them. In 2022, we made a big push to improve the way we talked to patients in our office—what we call our *verbiage.* The goal was not to "sell" to our patients but to help them understand why the products and services we were recommending were critical for their eye health. You'll learn more about what we actually changed in Chapter 8, but the bottom line is that we increased our revenue per exam by $32 that year.

Our total revenue increased by $365,000 from 2022 to 2023. $165,000 of that came from seeing more patients. But $200,000 of it came from better optical sales! In other words, from increasing our revenue per exam. We made an extra $200,000 just by changing the way we talk to patients! We didn't have to spend anything to make that. It didn't require any marketing efforts or ad spend or working a million hours to bring more patients into our practice. Actually, a lot of it came from just having longer conversations with our patients and getting to know them on a more personal level. It was fun!

As another example, I once worked with a doctor who wanted me to help make him more efficient. He was already seeing double the national average, but his revenue per exam was only $130 compared to the average of my clients, which is around $375–$400. You can probably see where this is going…

Rather than making him more efficient, I told him to basically do the exact opposite. I told him he needs to be *less* efficient. His patients weren't buying anything because he wasn't spending enough time with them, and he wasn't recommending good products. Of course they're not going to buy anything from you if you don't take the time to explain to them why they need the products you're recommending!

This is the bell curve I was talking about. If you're seeing too few patients, you're not making enough revenue. But if you're seeing too many patients, you may be holding yourself back by lowering your revenue per exam. There is a sweet spot, and that sweet spot will be different for every doctor. For me, it's about 12–13 exams per day. When I go over that, my revenue takes a hit because I'm not able to spend enough time with my patients and recommend the products they need. Your own sweet spot will depend on your communication style, but the best way to figure it out is to measure it.

This is why metrics matter. If you're not tracking these things, you'll never be able to optimize your revenue—you'll just be guessing and hoping things work out, which is not a great strategy.

Managing Growth

Before we dive into the specific metrics and how to think about them, I'd like to make one thing clear. Metrics aren't about "controlling" your growth, they're about *managing* it. I don't like the word controlling because it implies you're holding yourself back. I don't want to slow down or control my growth; I just want to manage it while growing as much as possible. Metrics will not control your growth; they will just give you the information to make informed decisions about where to focus your efforts.

You manage your growth, not your metrics. The metrics are just a tool to help you do that.

The other thing to keep in mind is that metrics are relative. If you were to ask me what number you should be shooting for on a specific metric, my answer would once again be "it depends." Don't try to match your percentages against norms or get hung up on trying to achieve a specific number. Every practice is unique, and the national norm may not apply exactly to your situation. Someone who practices in a more affluent area may have a higher cost of goods because they are selling more expensive frames, so the national norm doesn't really apply to them. What you're looking for is trends. Are your numbers trending in the right direction? Are the changes you're making having the impact you were looking for? That's what matters.

Alright, *now* we can get into the nitty-gritty. In the coming pages, we're going to review six key metrics:

1. Revenue per exam
2. Revenue per day (per doctor)
3. Revenue per patient
4. Total patient volume
5. New patient counts
6. New vs. established patient mix

After that, we'll cover some optical-specific patient growth metrics. The goal here is to understand each metric, what it means for your practice, and what affects it. In Chapter 6, we'll talk about how to turn these into decision-making tools. I promise I'll try to keep the jargon to a minimum. Let's get into it!

1. Revenue per Exam

This is one of the metrics that will give you the most valuable information about your practice. It's one of the most important ones to track, because it tells you how well you're helping patients understand the value of what you're recommending. It's a good indicator of practice health—if your revenue per exam is trending upward, that's a sign you're delivering quality care and developing great relationships with your patients.

Here's a good way to think about revenue per exam targets—although this comes with the big disclaimer that numbers are relevant depending on your location, size of practice, age of practice, etc. So don't have a panic attack if you're not within these targets.

- **Less than $325:** Far below average. (Patients are rarely buying what you're recommending.)

- **$325–$374:** Below average. (You could stand to make some improvements to how you talk with patients.)

- **$375–$424:** Average. (There's room to improve, but you're doing well.)

- **$425-$474:** Very good. (You're doing something right! Your patients are buying what you're recommending.)

- **Over–$475:** Excellent. (You're clearly providing high value and have a great relationship with your patients.)

The average from the practices I've seen in my coaching work is around $375. My own revenue per exam has ranged anywhere from $390–$440, depending on the year and the changes we've made to how we talk to patients. I've seen practices where it's as low as $170 or as high as $910.

The key thing to remember here is that the specific number isn't all that important. What's important is how it's trending. When I see this number declining, I know we need to work on our patient education or product recommendations. When I see it increasing, I know we're doing something right.

What affects this metric: Medical and specialty work will increase it (myopia management, dry eye treatment, etc.). Medicaid patients and heavy vision plan participation typically lower it. For this reason, some practices will track this metric with and without vision plan patients to get a clearer picture. The main influence you have on this metric is the way you talk to patients and how much they know, like, and trust you.

2. Revenue per Day (per Doctor)

This is a crucial metric to track as it can help you make projections and plan for what's next in your business. It's also directly related to both revenue per exam and exams per day. Increase either of those, and your revenue per day will go up. There is, however, a balance to consider.

If you do too many exams per day, your revenue per exam will take a hit, and you may lower your overall revenue per day. If you don't do enough exams per day, then your revenue per day will, of course, take a hit—even if you might be generating a lot of revenue per exam.

I've found that the sweet spot for most optometrists is around 12 to 14 exams per day. That's where you can maximize your revenue per day because you're dedicating enough time to each exam while still getting a lot of patients through the door. Personally, I've found that my own revenue per day actually *decreases* when I push past around 14 exams per day. Unless, that is, I get up to 16 or more exams per day, in which the number starts going back up. But that's exhausting for me, and I'd rather spend more time with each patient.

This is another metric that will vary greatly depending on your location and clientele. If you're in New York City and practically every person walking in your door is coming in for an eye exam and buying expensive frames, your revenue per day is going to look a lot different than a rural practice in a poor area. But a good target range is between $3,500 and $7,000 (or more) per day. I am currently at around $5,500 per day, and I do 13.5 exams per day on average.

My recommendation would be to track this metric for three months at a time, experimenting with different numbers of exams per day. See what happens to your revenue per day when you do fewer or more exams than where you're currently at. If you do that for three months at a time, you should be able to determine what makes sense for you.

Another reason to track this metric is to generate a baseline that you can use to make predictions or projections. As a quick example, let's say you typically generate $4,800 per day. If you want to take a week off, then you can expect around $24,000 in lost revenue. So you'd want to either figure out a way to generate that additional revenue or be prepared to add $24,000 onto the cost of your vacation. More on this in Chapter 6.

> **What affects this metric:** Primarily, your revenue per exam and number of exams per day. But there can be many other factors at play here, like insurance, staff efficiency, the hours you're open, and more.

3. Revenue per Patient

This is different from revenue per exam because it includes all those shorter visits, such as follow-ups, emergencies, contact lens checks, etc. It's helpful to track because it gives you a broader picture of how much you're generating from each person who walks through the doors of your practice. As you can imagine, it's helpful to know generally how much a patient is worth—you can use this to predict revenue growth as you accumulate more patients, create marketing budgets, and more.

For reference, my revenue per patient is around $175 to $200, while my revenue per exam is around $410.

What affects this metric: Your mix of exams versus all other appointments. Your scheduling efficiency can also affect this, if your short visits are affecting the number of exams you can schedule per day.

4. Total Patient Volume

This is everybody who walks through your door, no matter why they're there. I track both exams and encounters—*exams* are comprehensive eye exams, but *encounters* include contact lens checks, follow-ups, medical visits, all of it. You'll want to track this metric per day, which you can then use in combination with other metrics to gain a better understanding of how your practice is performing. Generally speaking, patients coming in for an exam are going to boost your revenue more than those coming in for other reasons.

One additional metric you might consider tracking within total patient volume is the percentage of patients who are coming in for exams versus encounters. At one point, I was seeing 28 patients per day, but only 10–12 of those were eye exams. That means less than half of the patients coming in my front door were getting comprehensive exams. That is not a healthy number. I have found that those who achieve 65–75% exams tend to have a better revenue per day and revenue per exam.

What affects this metric: Any marketing tactics that bring people into your practice, plus the number of follow-ups you're doing (which affects the percentage of exams versus encounters). The most common follow-ups tend to be dry eye, contact lenses, glaucoma, and macular degeneration.

5. New Patient Counts

This tracks people who haven't been in your office before or haven't been in for three years. I have a really simple way to track this. When we answer the phone, we ask everyone the same question: "When was your last exam here?" If they say "I've never been" or if it's been more than three years, they get logged as a new patient in our system. If they have seen us within the past three years, they are considered an established patient.

This is a metric you want to track on a monthly and yearly basis. For example, you should know how many new patients you acquired last month and last year. Then you can look at trends over time. Obviously, you want to be attracting new patients to your practice—but keep in mind this isn't the end-all be-all. If you're attracting lots of new patients but you're losing your established patients, that's not a great sign.

Which brings us to our next metric…

What affects this metric: Your marketing strategy, your culture, referrals, word of mouth—anything that will bring in new patients to your practice.

6. New vs. Established Patient Mix

Once you're tracking new patients, you'll want to keep an eye on the ratio between new patients and established ones. This is a really useful metric because it tells you about both marketing and retention.

New patients typically make up about 20% of our total patient volume. That means around 80% of our patients are established, which I'm pretty proud of. Generally speaking, 25:75 is a good ratio for most practices to shoot for. So that means 25% of your patients are new and 75% are established patients. Another way to think about it would be a 1:3 ratio—for every one new patient, you have three established patients.

Once again, context is key and you'll want to look at the trends here. If you've only been in business for two years, then you will have more new patients than a ten-year-old practice.

Your ratio may be well below 50:50, but that's fine. The important thing is that as the years go on, that percentage should ideally be decreasing. By year five, if you're close to that 25:75 ratio, you're doing great. If not, you just want to see the percentage of new patients decreasing over time.

> **What affects this metric:** Your culture, recall system, the way you talk to patients—anything that will bring patients back to your practice.

That wraps up the main performance metrics you should be tracking in your business. These will give you a good overview of how you're performing and let you create clear goals for improvement. As you make changes, you can review how these metrics change to figure out whether you're moving the needle in the right direction (or not).

Optical-Specific Metrics

Before we close this chapter out, I'd like to cover a few metrics that are more specific to optometry. These are helpful in understanding where your revenue is coming from. Revenue per exam is a great metric, but it does beg the question—where exactly is the revenue coming from? Is it contacts? Glasses? Transition lenses? Are people buying more than one pair of glasses? What about the mix between dailies and monthly contact lenses—is that having an effect on your revenue?

These are all questions that can be answered with the right data. When it comes to optical-specific metrics, I'm referring to:

- Capture Rate
- Annual supply of contacts
- Dailies vs. monthlies
- Transitions
- Second pairs of glasses

Capture Rate

Capture rate is the percentage of glasses you sell compared to comprehensive exams. It's one of the biggest indicators of how well you're helping patients understand their options. If someone needs glasses and you do your job right, they should be buying those glasses from you. If they're going elsewhere, that's not ideal for you and probably not ideal for them, as we all know the type of quality they can expect from certain name brands.

If you do 100 comprehensive exams and sell 55 pairs of glasses, your capture rate is 55%. This is an important metric to be aware of since optical sales typically represent the largest portion of revenue from each patient visit. You also have *a lot of* control over this. The way you talk to patients, your optical selection and pricing, and how well your optical team works with your patients—that all factors in. We'll talk more about those systems later.

The national average for capture rate is around 50–55%. However, it's important to understand that this number varies significantly based on your practice type. For example, our capture rate is lower than what you might expect because we're in a poor rural area where the nearest ophthalmologist is 45 minutes away. I get five to seven patients a day from the local clinic or emergency room who aren't there for glasses at all. Compare that to an optometrist in New York City, where their capture rate might be higher because more patients are coming in for a glasses exam versus a medically-oriented exam. It's simple math; there are more ophthalmologists in NYC than in Newport, TN.

If you're a highly medical clinic, 40% might be excellent for you. If you're basically just doing glasses exams all day, then maybe you should be at 75–80%. In our practice, we were hovering around 30% for a while until we brought in an optical consultant. After that, we got it to around 50%, which is pretty great for us.

Like with all these metrics, comparing yourself to national norms is helpful, but it is not the end-all be-all. You need to understand your own practice and what makes sense for your unique situation. A rural medical practice will naturally have a lower capture rate than an optical shop in an urban area where there are ophthalmologists on every street corner.

Annual Supply of Contacts

Annual supply of contacts refers to selling patients a full year's worth of contact lenses at once, rather than monthly or quarterly. This is more convenient for patients and it provides a better cash flow for your practice, so it's a win-win. You'll want to track what percentage of your contact lens sales are annual versus monthly or quarterly, and try to increase that percentage.

Now, there are a few reasons why annual supply matters beyond just convenience and cash flow.

The first is that we're all battling online competitors these days. There are a lot of people out there who are constantly looking for the best deals online, and frankly, it's hard for most of us to beat those deals (although rebates can help a lot with this). Getting a patient to commit to an annual supply of contacts means they have everything they need for the year, so they won't have a reason to go searching online for contacts.

The second reason is due to something called *the pantry principle.* Studies show that people who get an annual supply of contacts are much more compliant about wearing them correctly, and it makes perfect sense. Think about it this way: if you have 100 of something in your pantry and only two of something else, which one are you more likely to use? The one you have plenty of, right? The same principle applies to contact lenses. When patients have their full annual supply on hand, they're much more likely to replace them on schedule and come back for their annual exam when the time comes.

You already know what happens when people don't have enough on hand. The first three pairs of monthlies are actually replaced every month. The fourth one stretches to two months. The fifth becomes a quarterly. And by the sixth one, they can barely stand to wear it anymore because they've stretched it so long!

One important thing to note here is that when you increase your annual supply percentage, your cost of goods sold will go up—and that's actually a good thing in this case. It means you're doing more business and providing better care for your patients. We'll go deeper into cost of goods in the next chapter.

Another thing to keep in mind is that annual supply can be difficult in lower-income areas where people may not be able to afford purchasing a year's worth upfront. The industry average for this metric is around 25–30%, but that may vary depending on your location and clientele.

Dailies vs. Monthlies

As the name implies, this metric tracks the breakdown between how many daily disposable contact lenses you sell in your practice versus monthly contact lenses. Dailies typically generate more revenue per patient over time, and they're also healthier for most patients since there's less risk of infection and complications. In Chapter 8, I'll give you a great script for how to handle this conversation with patients. For now, just be aware that this is something you should be tracking, and that dailies tend to be better for both your business and your patients.

This is another situation where your cost of goods may go up as you convert more patients from monthlies to dailies, and that's fine. You're going to be paying more upfront for those daily lenses, but getting more when they're sold, which means more profit in the end. But again, you're not just doing this for profit—it really is the best option if you're looking to prioritize your patients' ocular health. (Which you should be!)

Transitions

I'm sure you're aware of what Transitions lenses are. This metric tracks what percentage of your glasses sales include Transitions lenses. It's often one of the easier add-ons to recommend because most patients can immediately understand the convenience factor—one pair of glasses that works both indoors and outdoors. It's also, once again, better for their eye health! If you wear glasses but you don't have prescription sunglasses, guess what? You're probably not going to wear sunglasses very often—and that is not good for your eyes. Transitions are a simple way to improve a patient's eye health while improving their quality of life at the same time.

The overall average for Transitions is around 50%, but independent practices tend to be closer to 35%. That gap probably comes down to patient education. When patients understand how Transitions work and the convenience they provide, they're usually interested.

Second Pairs of Glasses

This tracks the percentage of patients who purchase more than one pair of glasses. This might be computer glasses, sunglasses, a backup pair, or different styles. Second pairs of glasses are a great way to boost your revenue per exam, but it can be a challenging conversation to have in the exam room.

The industry median for second pairs of glasses is around 10%, while the average is more like four to five percent. What that tells me is that there is a small portion of doctors who are doing really well with this, and most doctors are not doing quite so well. I would say a good target to shoot for is around 15–20%—if you can manage that, you're doing great. The key here is identifying specific needs. I might ask a patient, "Do you work at a computer all day?" If they answer yes, then I might ask if their eyes bother them at the end of the day. When they inevitably say yes, I can start to talk about how computer glasses can solve that problem and why they're actually beneficial for their eye health. A lot of this, as you'll see in Chapter 8, starts to come naturally when you just get to know your patients. If I know the patient sitting in front of me is a big fisherman, I'm going to let him know that polarized prescription sunglasses will make fishing a whole lot more enjoyable. Not to mention, improve his eye health! Do you ever have patients who just keep breaking their glasses? Well, a second pair might be helpful!

If you're not already tracking this metric, you should be.

Understanding What the Numbers Really Mean

Now that you know what metrics to track and what they all mean, here's an important lesson. These metrics don't exist in isolation—they are all interconnected, and understanding the relationships between them is really what's going to add the most value to your practice. Otherwise, you're just collecting data for the sake of collecting data.

For instance, you might have a high revenue per exam but low patient volume. That could mean you're providing excellent care and education to the patients you see, but you might have capacity for more patients. Conversely, high volume with low revenue per exam might indicate you're rushing through appointments and missing opportunities to provide better care for your patients and increase your practice's business performance.

Metrics are also nuanced. There are many, many factors that go into certain numbers. I've given you some general trends to think about, but every situation is unique. For example, if you're a medical-heavy practice, your capture rate might be lower than most. Does that mean you're bad at talking to patients? No, it's probably low because most of your patients are simply at your office for medical reasons! It's important to think through your metrics and look at them from all angles.

I Love Google Sheets (And You Should Too)

Okay, one more thing before we move on. If you've been getting increasingly anxious about the amount of math in your future, please don't worry. You do not need to do math to track these numbers, and you don't need to be a wiz with spreadsheets.

You do, however, need one place to look at all your metrics and make sense of them. A spreadsheet tends to be the best way to do that—and luckily for you, I've included a bunch of spreadsheet examples on my website (www.DrKurtSteele.com) that you can download.

Personally, I love spreadsheets, and I've spent probably too many hours tinkering with mine to get them to a place where they are useful and make perfect sense to me. You can now benefit from that work—all you need to do is download the template and start plugging in your numbers. The spreadsheet will tell you everything you need to know about trends, comparisons, and projections. My accountant has even made our P&L match our expense metrics, so all I have to do is print it out, and I have everything I need in one place.

Someone could ask me right now what my cost of goods was in the second quarter of 2023, and I could tell them in three minutes. Most optometrists would take weeks to answer that question—they'd have to wait for their accountant to provide it, and then the P&L is often all over the place with no rhyme or reason to its organization.

Now, if working with spreadsheets isn't your thing or you want to make it even easier, I also work with optometrists one-on-one to help them set up and understand their metrics. We can walk through everything together, customize the systems to fit your practice, and I can help you interpret what the numbers are telling you. You can learn more about private coaching at my website as well.

However you decide to do it, having all your metrics in one place—a spreadsheet, scorecard, dashboard, whatever you want to call it—is essential because it helps you identify trends. I've been saying over and over again how the numbers themselves often aren't that important; it's the trends you should really be paying attention to. If you have everything in one place and you keep an eye on those metrics over time, you will naturally start to see the trends.

Tracking metrics will also show you how changes in your practice are affecting your growth in real time. I can tell you I've literally watched my revenue per exam go up after training my team on how we talk and follow up with patients. I can also tell you that knowing my metrics has helped me avoid some silly mistakes.

In 2024, for example, my personal total revenue actually went down by about $76,000 compared to 2023. Now, if I were just looking at total revenue, that would be pretty concerning. But when I looked at the metrics, I started to see the bigger picture.

First, I worked 10 fewer days in 2024 than I did in 2023. At my average revenue per day of about $5,500, those lost days accounted for $55,000 in lost revenue right there, nearly two-thirds of the full amount.

Second, in 2023, I was doing 13.9 exams per day and seeing 26 patients per day. In 2024, I thought I'd make up for those lost days by doing more exams when I was there, so I increased to 15.5 exams per day while still seeing 26 patients per day. I added an exam and a half per day, thinking that would help.

Instead, my revenue per day actually went down by $100, and my revenue per exam dropped by about $60. So the other $21,000 in lost revenue actually came from trying to do too much. When I pushed past my sweet spot of around 14 exams per day, I didn't spend enough time with each patient. I rushed through exams, didn't educate patients as well, and my revenue per exam ultimately went down.

The metrics showed me that trying to make up for fewer days by cramming in more exams actually hurt my bottom line. This also confirmed that my sweet spot is 13 to 14 exams per day. That's where I can maximize my revenue because I'm dedicating enough time to each patient while still maintaining good volume.

Without tracking these metrics, I might have thought the solution was just to cram more exams in fewer days. Instead, the data showed me that I just needed to go at my normal pace, and the only way to increase revenue was to work more days in the office.

That's just one example of why this stuff matters. I know tracking metrics isn't fun and that you probably don't want to spend what little free time you have looking at numbers, but it's worth it to keep things running smoothly. And if you want to grow your practice, it's mandatory. The time you invest into tracking metrics now will save you time in the long run because they'll help you make better decisions and avoid mistakes. These are tools to help you build the practice you want.

In the next chapter, we'll cover the other side of the equation: expense metrics. Because, as my dad used to say, "You can't just bring money in—you have to control what goes out." Once you understand both your performance and your expenses, you'll be well-equipped to start making smarter decisions about your practice.

Key Takeaways

1. **If you can't measure it, you can't manage it.** You have to run your business by the numbers. If you are not using numbers, you are running on emotions and gut feelings—and that is not a recipe for success. Tracking performance metrics is the first step in moving from guessing to informed decision-making.

2. **Revenue per exam and revenue per day are two important metrics to track.** Every metric from this chapter is important, but these two are some of the most useful. Revenue per exam is a great indicator of how you're performing as a business and the quality of care you are delivering for your patients. Revenue per day can be used to create projections and budgets, which will help you make decisions later on.

3. **Track trends, not just totals.** Don't obsess over hitting specific numbers, and don't beat yourself up if you're not near the national averages. Instead, focus on whether your metrics are trending up or down over time and monitor how changes in your practice affect the numbers. Remember, context is key.

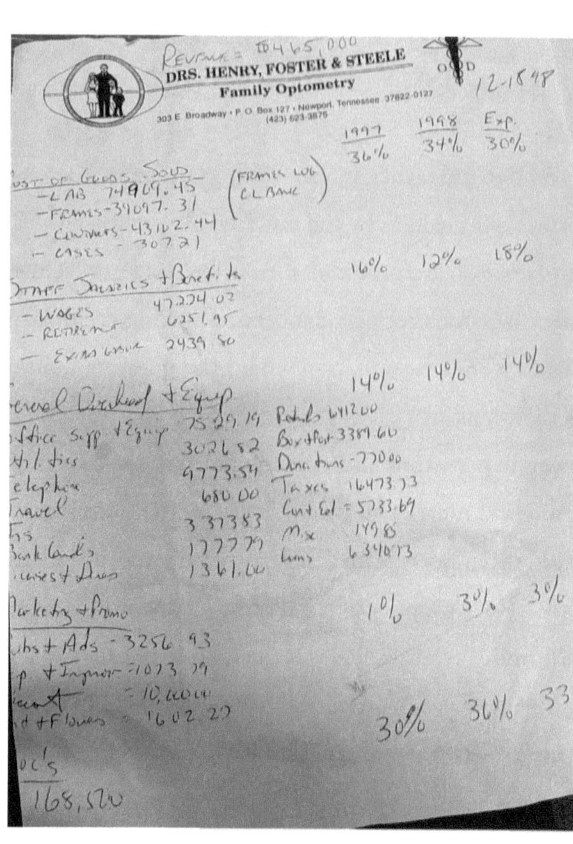

The original goal sheet!

5.
Expense Metrics

My dad was a chief operating officer, and he would often be brought in to help businesses that were facing difficulties. His strategy was simple—find the dead weight, get rid of it, and double down on what was working.

What that usually meant was making the hard decisions that the existing leadership had been avoiding. He would come in and implement a clear system of accountability that would expose the people who weren't contributing. Typically, he would discover that about a third of the staff were doing nothing and the other two-thirds were doing everything. And often, they didn't want to get rid of those people because they liked them or they had been with the company for a long time.

To my Dad, the solution was simple. Remove the people who weren't pulling their weight, then give raises to the performers. He was able to quickly reduce expenses while increasing productivity. But that solution wasn't so simple for the people running the company, since they had their own biases. They couldn't look at the situation objectively.

I remember one company where he had to fire 25 people just to keep the place from going under. That's an extreme example, and actually, most of his situations were pretty extreme, but watching him work and hearing his philosophies on business did teach me the importance of keeping expenses low.

In this chapter, you guessed it, we'll be covering expense metrics. Unless your practice is about to go bankrupt, you shouldn't need to worry about firing people or drastically cutting your expenses tomorrow. The idea is to use these metrics to control what goes out and find areas to save money. Tracking a few expense metrics and keeping an eye on what you're spending is an easy way to save a few thousand dollars per month, or maybe even more. And while you can delegate a lot of this, you as the business owner still need to be aware of what's going on and have systems in place to keep your expenses from getting out of control. The way to do that is through metrics.

You already know the drill, so I'm going to keep the chit-chat to a minimum here and get right into it. Just like last chapter, we'll start with a list of basic expense metrics that you should be tracking and their definitions. And just like last time, you can also find these on my website—www.DrKurtSteele.com.

EXPENSE METRIC DEFINITIONS

Cost of Goods Sold: The total cost of everything you buy that is for sale to the patient. Usually dominated by lens lab costs, contact lenses, and frames.

Staff Salaries and Benefits: The total cost of everything you spend on your non-OD team. (When I say "staff," I am always referring to your non OD team. Everyone but the doctors!) I also take out janitorial services and building maintenance services and put those in Overhead and Occupancy, respectively.

Staff Revenue per Hour: Revenue, as defined previously under performance metric definitions (actual bank deposits) divided by total hours on payroll. (Do not count ODs, janitorial services, or building maintenance. This is clinical/ office non-OD hours.)

Staff Cost per Hour: Total staff salaries and benefits divided by total payroll hours.

Revenue to Staff Cost ratio: Staff Revenue per hour, divided by staff cost per hour. (You want this between 4:1 and 5:1.)

Overhead: All indirect costs and expenses to operate the practice that cannot be directly attributed to any of the other categories. This typically includes things like:

- Professional fees
- Bank card fees
- Computer expenses
- Entertainment
- Insurance
- Lawncare and cleaning services
- Licenses and permits
- Office supplies
- Dues and subscriptions

Occupancy: Anything related to the structure you are practicing in. This includes but may not be limited to: rent, utilities, building maintenance, and property taxes.

Patient Care: Anything you've purchased to take care of the patient that is not for sale. Usually, monthly equipment leases dominate this category.

Marketing: Anything you've spent on marketing or advertising efforts. I include charity in this as well.

Optometric Doctor (OD) Compensation: Anything paid to partners or employed ODs. This is usually broken into two categories: salaries and benefits.

Cash Flow: Your profit, or whatever is left over at the end of the year. This typically flows into two buckets: Ownership compensation and cash on hand. The amount that flows into each will depend on where you're at in your

> practice, your goals, and whether you're looking to borrow
> money soon.
>
> **Ownership Compensation:** You and your partners'
> take of the cash flow. In other words, your compensa-
> tion for taking on the risk of ownership!
>
> **Cash on Hand:** The money in your checking account
> (liquid cash) and your rainy-day fund (we use a
> money market fund).

What Banks Expect

Before we dive into each of these metrics, one important thing to be aware of is how banks will interpret your metrics. You may already be aware of this, but I want to cover it because this is very important for growing practices and doctors who are looking to open new locations or expand.

If you ever want to get a loan for your business, you'll need to make sure your expenses are under control. Now, for the most part, banks are going to be looking at your cash flow and cash on hand. They want to know that you will be able to pay them back, so if you are consistently generating a decent profit and keeping a portion of that on hand, that tells them you'll have money to pay them, which is really all they care about.

If you have great cash flow, the other expenses won't actu-ally matter all that much in the eyes of the bank. If you don't have great cash flow, that's when they might look more closely at your other expenses. So both are important, but cash flow really is king.

The other reason to care about these numbers is that because banks lend lots of money to optometry practices, they know what a healthy practice looks like. Even if you're not planning to borrow money any time soon, these are just good guidelines to follow. If you can stay within these parameters, chances are you're doing pretty well for yourself. (This comes with the usual disclaimer that every practice is different, but you get the idea.)

Here's what most banks expect to see from a healthy practice (I actually got these targets directly from Chase, Bank of America, and Capital One):

- **Cost of Goods Sold:** 28%
- **Staff Salaries and Benefits:** 22–25%
- **Overhead:** 7–9%
- **Occupancy:** 8–10%
- **Patient Care:** 4%
- **Marketing:** 1%
- **OD Compensation:** 15–17%
- **Cash Flow:** 6–15% (which will then be split into ownership compensation and cash on hand, at varying percentages depending on where you're at and your priorities)

Now, obviously, every bank is different, and context is key. These aren't rigid rules that will apply in every situation, but if you're way outside of these ranges, it's worth asking yourself why. Maybe you're in a high-rent area and your occupancy costs are naturally higher. Maybe you've made a strategic decision to invest more heavily in advertising. Or maybe there actually is a problem under the hood and you need to look into it.

One key thing to understand is the value of cash flow and keeping some cash on hand. When you turn a profit at the end of the year, you can do whatever you want with that money. You might be tempted to distribute it all between you and your partners, and you could very well do that. But keep in mind that banks are expecting you to save some of that, whether it's just cash on hand that's sitting in a checking account or a rainy-day fund.

I learned this lesson the hard way when we wanted to make Emily a partner in our practice. We had been working with the same bank for *65 years,* so we had what I would call a long-term relationship with them. Now, you'd think that after all that time they would lend to us at the drop of a hat, but that was not the case. When we went to them to borrow money for Emily to be able to buy into the practice, they denied us because our cash on hand wasn't in the range they wanted to see. It took us two years to get that money.

This happened because Dr. Foster and I used to run the practice with essentially zero cash on hand. Every year on

December 31st, we would just pay ourselves everything that was left over—in other words, our entire cash flow was going to ownership compensation, and we weren't keeping any cash on hand, either in our checking account or a rainy-day fund. That worked great for us, but the bank didn't like it.

To them, it was a big red flag because they want to know that you have a cushion and you're not living paycheck to paycheck. We weren't living paycheck to paycheck, of course, and we could've just taken money out of our personal accounts if we had an emergency. But because that money was in our personal bank accounts and not on our practice's books, the bank couldn't see it. In their eyes, we're just scraping by every year, barely making ends meet, with no safety net or rainy-day fund.

If we had just known this ahead of time, we could've easily adjusted our cash flow by lowering our own compensation and keeping a portion of that cash flow on hand. But we hadn't done that, and frankly, they weren't going to budge—so we had to spend two years building up that cushion before they would lend us the money.

That's just one example of why this stuff matters. But generally speaking, if the bank considers you a healthy practice, then you are probably a healthy practice! So these are good benchmarks to shoot for.

Managing Expenses

Alright, it's time to dive into each expense metric. Even if you're already well aware of most of these, I would encourage you to keep reading. You might find some new insights or examples that will help you look at this metric in a new way. And if you really can't stand this stuff and want to just move on, that's okay too—next chapter is all about how to use these metrics to make better decisions.

1. Cost of Goods Sold (COGS)

Cost of goods sold (COGS) is everything that you plan to sell to patients, such as frames, contact lenses, sunglasses, Transitions, and anything else that goes directly to the care of your patients and generates revenue.

COGS should typically run around 28% of your total revenue. If you're significantly higher than that, you might be paying too much for your products or not pricing them appropriately. If you're significantly lower, you might be missing opportunities to offer better products to your patients.

One thing I learned early on is that COGS is an area where a lot of doctors try to save money in the wrong ways. They'll negotiate every penny with their lab or try to find the cheapest frames possible. But then their patients are unhappy because they're getting low-quality frames, and they don't come back!

Obviously, saving 2% on COGS isn't worth it if it makes your patients unhappy.

Therefore, the goal shouldn't be to minimize COGS—it's to optimize COGS. You want to buy quality products that your patients will love, at a price that allows you to maintain healthy margins. Remember the doctor I mentioned in the last chapter who practiced in a high-net-worth area? Her COGS is significantly higher than most, but that's okay because her patients are looking for high-quality, expensive frames. She might spend more on frames than the average doctor, but she's selling them for more as well. Context is key.

2. Staff Salaries and Benefits

This probably comes as no surprise given what we covered in Chapter 2, but this is one of the most important expense metrics. And unlike other expenses, I believe this is one where you shouldn't necessarily keep costs low. I would look more at your revenue per hour/cost per hour and keep that ratio between 4/1 to 5/1.

Banks expect staff salaries and benefits to be around 22–25% of revenue, but I think you should be on the higher end of that (assuming you have the right people). Our staff salaries and benefits typically run at around 24% of revenue, but we have to perform well in all other metrics to make this work.

I've talked at length about why you should hire great people and pay them well. Great people will generate far more revenue than the cost; they will make your life easier, make your practice more enjoyable—the list goes on. The reason why we can run our staff salaries and benefits at 24% is because we have great people who help us keep all our other metrics (performance and expense) in great shape.

On hiring someone new, let's say you are bringing in someone and their cost is $20 per hour. As we will learn in the upcoming text, we want at least a 4:1, if not a 5:1 ratio on revenue per hour/cost per hour. So ultimately, you want to somehow have a new hire result in $80-$100/hour in increased revenue. Now, not all of your expenses go up just because you hired someone, so this is not absolutely necessary to justify a new hire, but it is a good goal.

3. Occupancy

Occupancy includes rent, utilities, building maintenance, property taxes, and anything else related to the physical space where you practice. Banks expect this to be around 8–10% of revenue.

Now, if you're in Manhattan or San Francisco, your occupancy costs might be higher than 10%, and that's okay. But if you're in rural Tennessee like me and you're spending 15% on occupancy, you probably either have too much space or you're paying too much rent.

In the next chapter, we'll talk about how you can use this metric to make decisions around when to expand your practice to a bigger location.

4. Overhead

Overhead includes all indirect costs and expenses to operate your practice that cannot be directly attributed to any of the other categories. This typically includes things like computer expenses, office supplies, software subscriptions, insurance, continuing education, and professional fees.

Banks expect overhead to be around 7 to 9% of revenue. This is one area where you do want to be careful about overspending, but you also need to be smart about it. For example, I see a lot of doctors who try to save money by using outdated practice management software or using slower technology, sacrificing speed to save a few pennies. My Dad used to say, "Pinching pennies to lose nickels." In other words, if better software helps your team be more efficient or continuing education helps you provide better patient care, those are worthwhile expenses. Actually, they're not expenses at all—they're investments!

The key with overhead is to be intentional. Every expense should serve a purpose. If you can't explain why you're spending money on something and how it benefits your practice, it's probably time to cut it.

5. Patient Care

This category includes everything you use to take care of patients that you don't sell—mainly diagnostic equipment leases and maintenance contracts. Banks expect this to be around 4% of revenue.

This is an area where a lot of doctors either underspend or overspend. Neither one is great. Underspending means you don't have the equipment you need to provide great patient care. Overspending means you're buying every new piece of equipment that comes out, whether you need it or not.

The main problem I've noticed is that equipment companies are really good at selling, and optometrists love fancy new technology. The equipment reps will show you all the fancy features and tell you exactly how much you can bill Medicare if you buy their machine. They'll say things like, "If you do four tests a month, you'll make your money back!" It sounds great, but that doesn't necessarily mean you should buy it.

Before I buy any piece of equipment, I ask myself one simple question: *If I run this test, will the result affect the treatment of the patient?* If the answer is no, I don't buy it. It's that simple.

I've bought a couple of different types of glaucoma equipment, for example, and I didn't end up using them long-term because the results didn't make any difference in my treatment of the patient. I'd look at the results and think, "Okay, I'm going to do the exact same thing I would have before I got this machine." Those were not great investments.

If a piece of equipment helps you provide better treatment or makes you more efficient, that's good for patients and good for business. If it's just the latest gadget that looks cool but doesn't improve outcomes, then you probably don't need it. (As much as you might want it!)

6. Marketing

In a typical optometry budget, you may see this section referred to as "advertising," but really, advertising is just one strategy within the overall marketing umbrella. At a high level, marketing includes any money you spend to attract patients. So that might include advertising—like paid ads on social media, a billboard, or flyers—but it can include other things like sending promotional emails to your current patients or managing social media accounts.

I also include charity work in this category because it's a form of community investment that builds goodwill for your practice. Sponsoring a Little League team or supporting a local charity event often generates more patient referrals than traditional advertising.

The key with marketing is to track your return on investment. If you're spending money on advertising that doesn't bring in new patients, for example, stop doing it. If you find something that works, do more of it. You can't expect to just spend money on any random marketing tactic and have it work out. You need to keep track of your ROI and adjust your plan accordingly. Something that worked last year might not work this year, and you need to be prepared for that. Marketing is always a moving target.

7. Optometric Doctor (OD) Compensation:

Optometric doctor compensation includes salaries and benefits for all the optometrists in your practice, including you! Banks expect this to be around 15–17% of revenue.

Now, if you're a solo practice owner, this number might be higher because you're only paying yourself. I know what you're thinking: "Wouldn't it be *lower* because I'm only paying myself?" Yes, your total OD compensation would be lower, but your OD compensation as a percent of revenue would be higher. Why is that? Because having more doctors on your team makes you more money! When you add more doctors, you are benefiting from their productivity and generating additional revenue.

I find that many practice owners are too conservative with OD compensation, similar to staff salaries and benefits. They're afraid to pay market rates because they think it will hurt their bottom line. But if you pay below-market rates, you'll struggle to attract and retain good doctors, which will hurt your practice in the long run.

The key is to structure compensation in a way that incentivizes productivity. If doctors are generating revenue, they should be compensated well, and they should understand how their performance impacts their pay. If they're not generating revenue, you need to figure out why. We'll discuss how this all works when we talk about bonus systems in the next chapter.

8. Cash Flow

As a general disclaimer, you will see all sorts of definitions for cash flow. This is mine, based on talking to those in banking. I will be using this definition for the purposes of this book. Cash flow (also known as profit) is what's left after you've paid for everything else. Now, it's important to keep in mind that your cash flow is *not* your salary or take-home pay. Your compensation as an OD should already be accounted for in the OD Compensation category (unless you are an owner, then depending on your situation, some of the money you will pay yourself will be in this category). The best way to think about cash flow is that it's your cushion, emergency fund, growth fund, and reward for being an owner all rolled into one.

Cash flow primarily flows into two buckets in our office: **ownership compensation** (you and your partners' cut of the profit) and **cash on hand** (the primary checkbook and your rainy-day fund). That's not to say those are the only two things you can do with your hard-earned profit, but if you've set up the rest of your budgets correctly, you really shouldn't need to use this money for anything else. For example, while you could technically use your cash on hand to buy a new piece of equipment, that money should really be coming out of your patient care budget.

How much you pay out in ownership compensation and how much you save as cash on hand is up to you, and will depend on the health of your practice and if you're looking to borrow money soon. If you're not going to borrow money anytime soon and the checkbook looks good, then by all means, let the partners eat! Take your money and enjoy it. That said, I typically recommend holding on to 3–5% of your overall revenue as cash on hand, with some of it staying in the checkbook as liquid cash and some going into a rainy-day fund. For rainy-day funds, I'd suggest using a money market fund so you can get some return without any risk.

So if your cash flow is at 8%, you might save 3% as cash on hand, and the other 5% goes to you and your partners. If you want to be more conservative, maybe hold on to 5% and give 3% to you and your partners. That decision is up to you.

Now, in theory, you want your cash flow to be as high as possible, but in practice, that's not necessarily the best way to think about it. As we've seen, some of your expenses are more like investments for long-term growth. If you keep costs as low as possible, your cash flow will look great and you'll be doing well on paper. But if that comes at the cost of an unhappy team, unhappy patients, poor care for your patients, and inefficiencies, it doesn't really matter. You'd be far better off spending more money in those areas, as it will be more beneficial for the long-term health and growth of your practice.

Having some cash on hand is particularly important, both in the eyes of the bank and because it gives you breathing room. It allows you to handle unexpected expenses, like a piece of equipment breaking down. It also protects you from a lull in patients that might be outside of your control. This is why the bank is so concerned about cash on hand. They want to know that if something goes wrong, you will still be able to not only pay them, but keep your business afloat.

Some practice owners think they're smart by minimizing cash flow—in other words, keeping their expenses so low and paying themselves so well that they have very little profit on paper. The problem with this approach is that it makes you vulnerable, and you might miss out on opportunities.

Accidents happen, and you need to be prepared for that as a business owner. Banks understand this, which is why they want to see your cash flow at around 8–13% of total revenue. They want to know that you're making a profit, but they also want to make sure you're saving some of that profit for an emergency fund. That is exactly why the bank wouldn't lend us money when we wanted to make Emily a partner in our practice.

Balancing Expenses and Investments

At the beginning of this chapter, I told you how my dad would get rid of the dead weight when he was brought in to help a failing business. But even he would agree that you shouldn't always be trying to minimize expenses. I hope by now you've seen that expenses aren't just costs—they are often investments in your future growth. They are a necessary part of doing business.

Sometimes, keeping expenses low may actually be hurting your business. Sometimes high expenses may also be hurting your business. It's all about what you're spending your money on and what kind of return you're getting. When I decided to pay my staff more, for example, my staff salaries and benefits metric increased, but my revenue increased even more, which in turn made my staff salaries and benefits (as a percentage of revenue) go down. That investment has paid for itself many times over.

If you aren't already tracking the metrics we've just discussed, you should be. Remember that you can head to my website (www.DrKurtSteele.com) to download example spreadsheets showing how I recommend tracking everything. The goal should always be to have a dashboard where you can view all your key metrics in one place, and review that dashboard regularly to understand how changes in your practice affect the numbers.

One simple mindset shift I'd like you to embrace is to think of these metrics as potential opportunities. If you start tracking your metrics for the first time and you realize your occupancy rates are at 15%, for example, you shouldn't feel like you've made a big mistake. Instead, look at it for what it is: an opportunity to save money and increase your cash flow! If you really are at 15%, that's a sign that you are either not being efficient with your space or you're paying too much per square foot. Either way, you have an opportunity to either improve your efficiency or save money by finding a new, cheaper location (I suggest the first option, which is a lot more fun! Take your rent and divide it by .08. That becomes your new revenue goal!)

The point of this isn't to make you feel good or bad about your numbers; it's to make better business decisions and work smarter, not harder. Now that we're clear on all the core metrics you should be tracking, it's time to talk about how exactly that works. In the next chapter, we'll cover how you can use metrics to create budgets, forecasts, bonus systems, and inform big decisions like when to add more doctors or expand your space. This is going to be a good one.

Key Takeaways

1. **You can't just bring money in; you have to manage what goes out.** Great performance metrics mean nothing if your expenses are bleeding you dry. Balance is everything. As my dad taught me, sometimes you need to cut the dead weight and invest in what's working. The goal isn't to spend as little as possible—it's to spend strategically on things that generate returns while eliminating waste that drags you down.

2. **Use bank benchmarks as your guide, not gospel.** If your numbers fall outside the ranges a bank expects, ask yourself why. You might have good reasons, but you should be making those decisions consciously. Banks know what healthy practices look like because they see the numbers from thousands of businesses. If you're significantly outside their ranges, that's not necessarily bad—but it should be intentional, and you should understand exactly why your practice operates differently.

3. **Remember the importance of cash on hand.** Cash flow isn't just profit that you can add to your take-home pay. Keeping cash on hand is almost like another form of insurance for your business. It means you can weather unexpected challenges, invest in growth opportunities, and sleep better at night knowing you have a financial cushion when you need it most. Plus, having cash on hand is more or less mandatory if you want to borrow money.

6.

Data-Based Decision Making

———

"Holy crap, Kurt! We can't build this!"

That was Emily's reaction when I told her how much our new Greeneville office was going to cost. And I couldn't blame her, because it was a big number. We currently pay about $2,200 a month in rent for our current building, and the space is maxed out. We were planning to build a new 5,400 square foot facility that would give us room to grow and add another doctor.

When we first started talking to builders, we were looking at monthly payments of around $18,000. Based on our projections, I was convinced we could make that work. I was a big proponent for expanding—let's go ahead and do it!

Coincidentally, we actually received the final bid as I was writing this chapter… And it changed. A lot. Our builder just told us that the real price is now going to be *$25,000 per month*.

This is late 2025, and the price of materials has skyrocketed since we first started looking at this project. When I heard that new number, part of me felt like I should just go for it—we've already done all the planning, we've gotten the land approved, and we're ready to break ground. Let's just get this thing done. But instead, I pulled up my spreadsheets to run the numbers. I knew we could figure this out and come up with a better solution.

When we first started this project, Greeneville was doing about $1.4 million in annual revenue. I was convinced that with a new building and space to add a new doctor, we could turn that into a $3 million office. I remember telling Emily, "Look, $18,000 a month is $216,000 in annual rent. If we can get to $3 million in revenue, which I think we can, then our rent would be 7.2% of collections. That's right in line with where occupancy should be."

Now, at $25,000 per month, we're looking at $300,000 per year in occupancy costs. To keep that at a healthy 8% of revenue, we'd need to be doing $3.75 million annually. Even with a new doctor and better location, getting to $3.75 million would take years—and in the meantime, we'd be bleeding money on rent that was eating up over 20% of our revenue.

To me, the path forward was obvious—one way or another, we would need to get the monthly payments down. As of writing this, I just went back to the builder and said, "Look, we've done the math. We can't afford this at $25,000. It needs to be at $17,000–$18,000. How can we make that happen?"

We're now looking at building a smaller facility—around 3,000 to 3,500 square feet instead of 5,400—and maximizing our space with more up-to-date technology that takes up less room. Or we might wait a couple of years, pay down on the land, and build the larger facility when the numbers actually make sense.

Three weeks ago, we were planning on having a big new building that would be right in line with our target occupancy costs. Now, things have changed. By the time you're reading this, things may have changed again! That's okay. While I'd rather not have things change at the last minute, the reality is that material and building costs are outside of my control. However, I am in control of how I react to the situation.

Knowing the numbers allowed me to make that decision quickly and avoid what could have been a catastrophic mistake. If things change three weeks from now, I can look at the numbers and change our plan accordingly.

As a business owner, you will have to take risks. That's just part of playing the game. Sometimes, those risks can be pretty darn scary—this was one of them. But if you want to grow, you have to take certain risks. The key is removing fear from the equation by using data to make decisions with confidence. I've already done that with this new building multiple times, and I may have to do it again. If that happens, I'll be ready.

When I look back at my business (and life), most of the success I've achieved is a result of having the courage to take risks. Opening my practice, adding a new doctor, paying my team more, even going to optometry school in the first place—those were all risks that paid off big time.

In the beginning, I'll admit that I took some of those risks just based on wishful thinking—but I really started to experience success when I began making decisions based on numbers. Whether it's a decision about hiring someone new, buying equipment, or building a new location, there's always a plan—and that plan is always based on actual data, not hope or guesswork.

This chapter is all about using your metrics to make courageous decisions, even when they seem scary. This is what holds most business owners back from hitting that next level of success. They know they can do the work and make the tough decisions. The courage exists within them to do these things, but they need something to help them pull the trigger. Metrics and data will make that difference. Put simply, those scary decisions become a lot less scary when you have numbers proving they will work.

In the following pages, we're going to look at four examples of how you can use metrics to inform your decision-making, including:

1. Budgets and projections
2. A bonus system that actually works
3. When to add more doctors
4. When to expand your space

Much of this you'll be able to implement in your business right away. But beyond the tactical stuff, my ultimate hope is that you'll walk away from this chapter with a new perspective on what metrics can do for your business and how to use them to think through complex problems. Once you adopt a more numbers-focused mindset, you can start to logically work through problems in your business, and the solutions practically present themselves to you. And let me tell you, when you can do that, everything gets easier. (And less scary!)

Budgets & Projections

One of the easiest and most useful things you can do with metrics is use them to forecast what's going to happen in the future, then build budgets based on that. Most optometrists I meet tend to do the opposite. They get to the end of a quarter, look at what happened, and then try to build a budget for the next quarter based on what just happened.

It's not a terrible way to handle it, but there's a pretty obvious problem with this way of thinking. You're basing your Q2 budget on Q1, but those are two different quarters! You're just assuming they will be the same, but you don't know that. Rather than looking at what's happened in the past, I prefer to forecast what is likely to happen in the future.

Here's how it works. Every quarter, I have all my doctors do one simple thing: write down how many days they're going to work. That's it.

Once I have that number, we can then multiply it by each doctor's respective revenue per day. That becomes our projected revenue for the quarter.

Here's an example: Let's say you're a two-doctor practice that's pulling in about $1.4 million in revenue. You've calculated your average revenue per day to be around **$4,750,** and you know you're going to work **40 days** in the upcoming quarter. Your projected revenue for the quarter would then look like this:

$$40 \times \$4{,}750 = \$190{,}000$$

So now you know that you're going to bring in around $190,000 in the next quarter. And that's not just a guess—it's a pretty darn accurate number. Now, let's say your partner is also working 40 days that quarter and their revenue per day is $4,000. That's $160,000 from them.

Add those together, and your total projected revenue for the next quarter is $350,000. Now that you know that you'll have $350,000 to work with, you can apply the expense percentages we covered last time to create your entire budget for the upcoming quarter. Remember, each practice is unique! These are the percentages we use in my practice, and what we'll use in the example that follows:

- **Cost of Goods Sold:** 28%
- **Staff Salaries and Benefits:** 24%
- **Overhead:** 7%
- **Patient Care and Equipment:** 4%
- **Occupancy:** 8%
- **Marketing:** 1%

So if you're projecting $350,000 in revenue for the quarter, you can just apply those percentages to that number to get a budget for each category:

- **Cost of Goods (28%):** $98,000
- **Staff Salaries and Benefits (24%):** $84,000
- **Overhead (7%):** $24,500
- **Patient Care and Equipment (4%):** $14,000
- **Occupancy (8%):** $28,000
- **Marketing (1%):** $3,500

Wouldya look at that?! There's your budget for the quarter, done. The hardest part of that was just getting the number of days worked—once you have that, the calculations take a few seconds.

Implementing Your Budget With Your Team

Having a budget is one thing, but what you do with that budget is another. I find that many optometrists feel they need to personally be in control of every part of their budget. I don't recommend doing that. Why? Because you have much better things to spend your time on (like generating revenue), and because you can use budgets to give your team ownership over their departments.

For example, I've determined that most practices should be spending about 6% of their overall budget on frames. As a side note, this is one area that many practices overspend in—the two biggest budget drainers I tend to see are occupancy and frames. Some people have way too many frames.

Anyway, if you know you're going to bring in $350,000 this quarter, you can just calculate 6% of that, which is $21,000. Then, you can walk over to your optical manager and tell them: "You can spend $21,000 on frames this quarter."

That's it. That's all you have to do. In my practice, that is literally all I do, and I leave the rest up to my optical manager. She now knows exactly what she can spend and she can plan accordingly. If she wants to save a little money in month one to make a bigger purchase in month two, she can do that. But she has guardrails, and she knows that if she comes in under budget, that money goes into the bonus pool (more on that in a minute).

I can't tell you how nice this is, both for me and her. I *love* that I don't have to think about frames, and she loves that I am giving her ownership over her department! Plus, she deals with frames every day, so she is much better-equipped to figure out what to buy than I am. (Remember the story about everyone in Newport wearing the same round tortoise shell frame? Yeah, I'd like to avoid that.)

This type of thinking can be used in lots of different areas of your business. Another simple one is staff salaries. In our previous example, your staff budget for the quarter would be $84,000. Now, let's say your average staff cost is $22 per hour per person (this includes additional things like benefits, training, etc.). You can do some simple math to figure out how many hours per week your staff can work to stay within that budget:

$84,000 ÷ $22 per hour = 3,818 hours for the quarter

3,818 hours ÷ 13 weeks in a quarter = 293.7 hours per week

That's about 300 hours per week, or 7.5 full-time equivalents (FTEs). Now you know exactly how many hours of labor you can afford that quarter. If you're running over that, you know you need to make some adjustments. If you're running under, you might have room to hire someone new.

I just love this because it makes running your business *easy.* You don't have to be a genius. You don't have to have a degree in finance. You just need to know your revenue per doctor day, count your working days, and apply some percentages. The numbers literally make the decisions for you.

A Bonus System That Actually Works

I've talked at length about the value of paying your team well, and a big part of that can be done through a bonus system. Bonuses are great because they can be used to incentivize your employees, and they are typically only paid out as a result of having excess cash on hand. When your team understands the system and how they ultimately control the size of their bonus, they will naturally want to work hard and perform well. Best of all, you don't have to agonize over how much each person should get—once again, the numbers are making the decisions for you.

Our bonus system actually came out of a survey I did with my team, years ago. I wanted to know about their experience working with us, what we could improve, and what they wanted to get out of their jobs, so I just made a quick survey and sent it out to everyone. One thing that came up was that almost all of them wanted to know when they're doing a good job and when they're doing a bad job. They also wanted to feel like they had some control over their compensation. In other words, they wanted transparency.

We created two bonus systems that would help in both those areas—one for the team and one for the doctors. Both are based on the same principle: if you can control expenses while maintaining or increasing revenue, you get rewarded for it.

The Team Bonus System

For our non-OD staff, we focus on the expense categories they have the most control over, which are **cost of goods sold, staff salaries and benefits,** and **overhead.** In a typical practice, these three categories combined should be around 60% of your revenue. In my practice, we target 60%.

Here's how the bonus works: every six months, we look at those three expense categories. If the team has kept them at or below 58% of revenue (2% under our target), they get to split half of that 2% as a bonus amongst themselves. Basically, I'm telling them what our budget is, and if they can keep us under budget (without affecting revenue), they get to keep half of what's left over. Simple, right?

I'll give you an example of how this works with real numbers. Let's say we did $1,000,000 in revenue over a six-month period. Our target for cost of goods sold + staff + overhead is 60%, or $600,000.

But let's say the team did a great job. They managed costs well, didn't waste materials, controlled overtime, and worked really efficiently. At the end of six months, those three categories only totaled 58%, or $580,000.

That's a difference of $20,000. So the team gets to split $10,000 of that, and the practice keeps the other $10,000 (meaning it becomes part of our cash flow). For a team of 10 people, that's $1,000 per person, twice a year. Not bad. We do this at the end of June and end of December every year.

The best part about this system is that they are the ones who are in control of it. I'm not micromanaging our cost of goods sold. I'm not hovering over Stephanie, telling her what frames to buy. I give her a budget at the start of each quarter, and she knows that if she comes in under that budget while still meeting our patients' needs, it's going into the bonus pool.

That creates a completely different dynamic. Instead of me being the bad guy who has to tell people to spend less, they're motivated to work smarter because it directly benefits them. One example—Molly came to me one day and said, "Hey Kurt, I think we can actually move our billing and coding in-house. Here's what I was thinking..." We actually did that, and it saved us $90,000 per year. That's exactly the type of behavior I want from my team, and this bonus system is a great way to make it happen.

Recently, I was able to show how this works in real time when I was coaching a practice. Like I always do, I'd sent a survey to the staff asking what they wanted to improve before I arrived at the office. One of their main concerns was that their office furniture was outdated—they were actually embarrassed by how old everything looked. So on my last morning there, we went furniture shopping together. (Seriously!)

The doctor was prepared to spend about $4,000 to $5,000 on new waiting room furniture, which was more than she wanted to, but she trusted the process. We were standing in the furniture store, and the team had decided on the most expensive table in the place. I stopped them and said, "Y'all, this is a great teaching moment."

I turned to the doctor and said, "First of all, it's a shame that you even have to be here. You should be able to trust your team to handle decisions like this without you having to supervise." Then I looked at the team and explained the bonus system I was recommending they implement—where cost of goods, staff, and overhead directly affect their bonuses.

I pointed to another table across the showroom that looked nearly identical to the one they were about to buy, but it was $2,400 less. "Here's the question you need to ask yourselves," I said. "Is this table worth $800 out of each of your paychecks? Because that's what it's costing you."

They got the cheaper table.

The team went from spending someone else's money to making smart financial decisions with their own money. And the best part is that the doctor realized she didn't need to be there micromanaging furniture purchases—her team could handle it on their own if they understood how the decisions affected the business, and by extension, their bonuses.

That is why having a clear bonus system is so important. It motivates and incentivizes your team to do what's best for the practice, because that is what will ultimately improve their bonus. I sometimes joke about how I would love to come into my practice and see that my team had completely renovated the waiting area without telling me. Only it's not a joke! I don't want to have to deal with that myself, and if they did make any changes, I would know they were operating within our budget and keeping costs low to keep their bonuses high. When I talk about this with other optometrists, I always hear the same thing: "Oh my gosh, you're right—I would *love* that!"

The Doctor Bonus System

For the doctors, we use a similar system, but we focus on the expense categories that doctors have more control over, which are OD compensation, occupancy, patient care and equipment, and marketing. These four categories typically make up about 36–37% of revenue in our practice.

The partners and associate doctors have input on the equipment we purchase and our marketing decisions. The partners also determine or negotiate the rent and what each OD makes. So, we reward ourselves when we keep those expenses below target.

Using the same example, if we did $1,000,000 in revenue over six months and our target for these four categories is 36% ($360,000), but the doctors kept it at 34% ($340,000), then the partners get to split half that 2% difference or $10K. The non-partner ODs typically get 17% of collections in our practice, so we make up that difference every six months.

The reason these bonus systems work so well is that they create transparency and shared accountability (which is exactly what they were looking for in that initial survey). Everyone knows what the targets are, everyone can see the numbers, and everyone benefits when we hit our goals. It also gives them control. They don't have to come to me to make decisions about where to spend money; they just know that they have a certain budget to work with, and they can do with that what they will. I trust them implicitly—I'm available if they want to bounce ideas off me or ask questions, but for the most part I assume they can handle it on their own. (And they do!)

One thing we do is review these metrics together at our Fun Friday meetings. That way, everyone knows where we stand, and everyone knows what they need to do to earn their bonuses. I would definitely recommend doing something like that if you're going to implement a similar system—you need to make sure everyone's on the same page and understands the numbers.

It's not unusual for our staff to get \$10,000–\$12,000 to split among themselves over the course of a year. That's real money. That pays for vacations, pays down debt, and helps with Christmas shopping. It makes a difference in their lives. But it also makes them part of the business, and that's important. They know that they have a direct stake in our success, which changes a lot about how they show up to work. Our success is their success!

When to Add More Doctors

I've mentioned this before, but I'll mention it again because I hear it all the time: If you are booked one month out, that is a serious problem. That is not something you should be bragging about. No one wants to book an appointment a month in advance! If that's the case, they'll just go somewhere else instead or not come in at all (which is even worse). Plus, that probably means you're overworked just from trying to see everyone who needs you.

The solution to this problem is to add another doctor. As a general rule, if you are booking between three weeks to one month out, it's time to get some help. It's not only going to make your life easier, but it will also make the practice a whole lot more money.

The one other time it makes sense to hire another doctor is if you just want to slow down yourself. Maybe you've been working hard for 20 years and you're ready to see fewer patients, or you want to focus on more specialty care—that's a perfectly good reason to hire another doctor; you'll just want to make sure they are going to generate enough to cover what you're paying for, plus some breathing room.

About 15 years ago, I had a conversation with my financial advisor, Mark B. Murphy, that changed my perspective on all this. And by the way, I have to say that Mark is an absolute genius and I am so lucky to have him as my financial advisor. Mark told me, "Kurt, when it's time to add doctors to your practice, don't wait. Grow your business. *You* are your best investment." That was some of the best advice I've ever received.

Adding another doctor is one of the primary ways you can expand your business, but it's another one of those decisions that can be tough for many optometrists to make. It might feel like a big risk, but if you break down the numbers, you can start to see how it works.

Let's say you hire a new doctor and pay them 17% of collections. If you're netting 25% profit in your practice and they collect $600,000 in a year, you're going to make 25-30% of that just for having them there. You're literally making money while they're working—even after paying them fairly—and you're making your life easier as well. The reason you will make that percentage is because not every category is going to go up proportionally, so you will make more than just the net. For example, your occupancy will probably stay the same. So, increased revenue with a new doctor will make your occupancy percentage plummet! I won't get too deep into how this all works, just take my word for it!

Another thing to consider is that if you really are booked out one month in advance and you add another doctor, you can now see all those patients you were turning away. You can start accepting new patients again and grow your practice. Plus, you can take that vacation you've been putting off because you've been too busy! If you structure it right, that new doctor can also become a partner over time, which is how you build long-term wealth and create an exit strategy.

So let's take a look at how that works.

Making it Happen

When I bring on a new doctor, here's how I structure it. For the first 24 months, they're employed, but the purchase price for their partnership is already agreed upon upfront. We structure it so that when they become a partner instead of an employed doctor, they'll actually take home more money even after making their practice payments.

If you can't accomplish that—if the numbers don't work out so they're better off as a partner than as an employee—then your practice isn't ready to sell yet. You've got some work to do.

After those first two years, we do owner financing at the Applicable Federal Rate (AFR) to avoid "imputed interest" issues, and amortize it over 10-15 years depending on what the cash flow will handle. After three years they go to the bank for the final portion. This gives them time to prove themselves, gives me security, and gives them a path to ownership that doesn't require them to come up with hundreds of thousands of dollars upfront. It also proves to the bank that the cash flow works because they've already been paying you for three years.

One alternative is that the senior partner and the partner buying in can agree to refinance the remainder of the loan at prime minus 1% over seven to 10 years. This would save some taxes for the senior partner and make life easier because you don't have to go to the bank. The seven to 10 years can be used to either pay off the loan quicker or lower the monthly payment, whatever suits the senior partner and the partner buying in.

Now, getting the new doctor in is only half the battle. You need to get them some patients! I'm proud to say that every new doctor I've ever added was booked out over a week on day one because I simply gave them some of our patients. I've never understood the optometrists who add a young doctor and then only give them certain patients or keep them half-empty while they're booked out for four weeks. That makes no sense at all—I will happily give our patients to a new doctor because when they win, we all win. If they're producing revenue, they feel good because they're doing what they were hired to do and building relationships with patients. And I feel good because we're serving more patients and growing our practice! Plus, my current patients are happy because they can get appointments when they need them.

What's not to like?

When to Expand Your Space

Adding more doctors and expanding your space go hand in hand—in fact, oftentimes one will require the other. You might need to expand your space to add a new doctor, or you might need to add a doctor to make enough revenue for a new space to work (like we saw in the beginning of this chapter). So let's talk about how to know when you're ready for this.

The key to knowing when it makes sense to expand comes down to understanding two metrics: **revenue per square foot** and your **occupancy percentage.** When you track these numbers together, they'll tell you whether you've outgrown your current space or whether you need to find ways to be more efficient with what you already have.

The idea is simple. As your practice grows, you'll generate more revenue in the same amount of space. At a certain point, you physically won't be able to fit more patients or doctors into your current building. You'll need more exam rooms, more waiting room space, more storage for your optical department—you get the idea. If you're tracking your revenue per square foot, you should see that number increase over time as you grow your practice in your current space. But at a certain point, it will start to stagnate. When that happens, that is likely a sign that you've maxed yourself out—you're getting everything you can out of your current space and either need to expand or look for ways to use your space more efficiently.

Now, I used to have a target number for revenue per square foot that would indicate exactly when you were maxed out. But as you saw in the beginning of this chapter, things have changed quickly here. Frankly, that system became obsolete as I was writing this book because the cost of building materials and construction has skyrocketed so much.

Technology is now also changing things. With newer diagnostic equipment, you can actually do a full eye exam in a 6' x 6' room (36 square feet), which used to require at least 96 square feet of space. So instead of immediately jumping to expand your space, you might want to first invest in equipment that allows you to maximize the efficiency of your current location.

When you do look at expanding, however, the key is to make sure that your new building and projected revenue will keep your occupancy costs in that healthy 8–10% range we discussed in the previous chapter. If you've been tracking all your metrics, you can make projections to ensure this all makes sense.

For example, if you know your average revenue per day, you can calculate roughly how much you'd expect to make by bringing a new doctor in. With that, you could project your revenue for the new location and make sure that your building costs are in the 8–10% range, just like we did when deciding on our new Greeneville office.

As much as I would love to give you a one-size-fits-all formula here, it's just not feasible because things are changing so fast and each situation is unique. If you want help thinking through whether it's time to expand or how to maximize your current space, head to www.DrKurtSteele.com and let's talk. Understanding the basics of revenue per square foot and occupancy costs will help you start to think about this decision, but it's best handled on a case-by-case basis with someone who can look at your specific numbers and circumstances.

But remember, just because you can expand doesn't necessarily mean you should. I've seen many practices expand too early, and that is a recipe for a whole lot of stress. It happens all the time—people start growing and get overly excited, so they build or move to a much bigger space, only to have their revenue stagnate while their occupancy costs skyrocket. That is not a good situation to be in, so if you're going to expand, you need to have a plan in place.

If you are scared about expanding your space, that's probably just a sign that you need to get a better handle on your metrics and make some projections (and a plan) for where you're headed. When the numbers look good and you have a plan for how to make the most of your new space, that fear will disappear and you will have the courage to take the next step!

Putting It All Together

There are a lot of things you can do with metrics, and one thing that I think holds back a lot of optometrists (and business owners in general) is that they feel they need to understand every nuance of every metric and how they all relate. That couldn't be further from the truth. Really, you just need to understand a few key metrics and how to use them to make better decisions in your business.

The metrics we've discussed so far will give you a solid foundation—in fact, for most practice owners, there's not much else you'll need to track. If you, like me, enjoy this stuff and want to go deeper, then by all means go ahead. This is something I can also help you with in my coaching, where I can give more tailored advice based on your unique situation.

The biggest thing I'd like you to take away from this chapter is to just get started. Start tracking your metrics and spend some time every quarter reviewing them. It doesn't take long. Every quarter, I spend about an hour plugging my numbers into a spreadsheet, and after that hour, I can tell you:

- Exactly how much revenue we're on track to generate next quarter
- Exactly how much we can spend in each category
- Whether any of the changes I made in the past quarter have had an impact
- If there are any major red flags to be investigated
- How much my team is on track to receive in bonuses
- Whether it's time to consider hiring
- Whether it's time to consider expanding our space

In my experience, that is what most practice owners want to know—but they're not tracking the metrics that will give them that information, or they're not readily available. When I go into most practices and ask a simple question like, "What was your cost of goods last quarter?" I'm usually told that it will take a few weeks for their account to get back to them on the exact number. That's a problem the doctor should be able to pull up within a few minutes. That absolutely blows my mind! There's no way you can run a practice efficiently without being able to know those numbers and access them to make quick decisions within minutes.

If you're looking to put this all to use in your business, I would once again highly recommend heading to my website and looking at the example spreadsheets we have there. You can then build your own, or you can contact me at www.DrKurtSteele.com if you'd like further help. I figured this stuff out on my own, so if I can do it, you can too. The only difference is you get to skip all the mistakes I had to make in the process!

Having those numbers, being able to pull them up at a moment's notice, and actually *understanding* what they mean and how they relate to your performance is what will give you the courage to make the tough decisions required to build the practice you ultimately want.

The information we've covered up to this point will get you far, but there will always be obstacles in your way—that's just the way running a business works. Sometimes those obstacles are obvious—like an employee with a bad attitude or an expensive piece of equipment breaking down—but other times they are not so obvious. In the next chapter, we're going to cover some of the not-so-obvious ones. These are what I call the "silent killers," which are hidden profit drains that most optometrists don't realize are costing them thousands of dollars per year.

Key Takeaways

1. **Use data to remove fear from decision-making.** Big decisions like expanding your space, hiring new doctors, or increasing payroll can be scary—but when you have the numbers to back up your choices, you can make those decisions with confidence instead of relying on gut feelings or emotions.

2. **Metrics are tools, not report cards.** If you discover your occupancy is at 15% or your revenue per exam is below average, that doesn't mean you've failed. Those are opportunities to improve! Every "bad" number is simply showing you where you have the most room for improvement and growth, and sometimes even small changes will make a big difference.

3. **Situations change, so stay flexible with your approach.** What worked five years ago might not work today—building costs, technology, and market conditions evolve. Use the foundational principles (like revenue per square foot and occupancy percentages) to guide your thinking, but recognize when you need to adapt your strategy or seek case-by-case guidance for major decisions.

7.
The Silent Killers

We've spent the last few chapters talking about how to use metrics to track your performance, manage your expenses, and make better business decisions. But even with the best metrics, there are still things that can slide through the cracks. In my experience, most optometry practices have hidden profit drains that are quietly costing them thousands or even tens of thousands of dollars per year. These are things that won't show up on your metrics spreadsheets, and they're easy to miss.

I call these silent killers, and in this chapter, we're going to go over some of the most common ones out there.

What is a Silent Killer?

A silent killer is anything that affects your profitability without you realizing it—or at least, without you thinking it's important. These are the little things that add up to cost you money month over month. In isolation, these seem negligible, but over time, they can cause very real problems.

I've had plenty of silent killers in my business, and I probably still do—I just need to find them! But the big wake-up call for me happened a few years ago when I found out how much I had been giving away in what I call spiffs and freebies—basically, discounts for friends and family, and just generally being "too nice." Honestly, I'm kind of a bleeding heart, and I'll just give stuff to our patients sometimes—especially if I know they don't have much money.

I knew this wasn't great, so I had a team member keep track of every time I gave something away for free. Well, as it turned out, I gave away $8,000 of stuff over six months. $8,000! That's $16,000 a year, gone! Just given away. And I didn't even get to write it off as a donation.

Once I saw that number, I knew I had to put some systems in place to manage this. It also taught me an important lesson, which is that I can't just assume everything in my practice is running smoothly. Even though I was tracking my metrics and doing everything seemingly right, I still had to actively look for those silent killers and fix them.

The Most Common Silent Killers

In my work as a coach, I've seen the same silent killers pop up in most of the practices I work with. If you're not actively aware of these in your practice, there's a good chance they're costing you money right now.

The most common culprits are:

1. The Phone
2. No-shows, cancellations, late patients, and empty slots
3. Accounts receivable
4. Spiffs and freebies

The good news is that silent killers are one of those things where, once you see them, *you can't unsee them.* Usually, when I go into a practice and start looking around, I'll notice a few of these right away. The best part is that fixing them is typically quick, easy, and low-cost. So rather than thinking about these as problems, think about them as opportunities!

1. The Phone

Oh boy, this is a *big one.* One of the first things I do when I visit an optometry practice is ask about their phone system and even listen to how their receptionist answers the phone. Why? Because your phone is the lifeblood of your practice. Every call is an opportunity, which means that every missed call is a missed opportunity.

Think about your phone system right now. When someone calls your practice, what happens? Do they go to an automated system, or do they immediately talk to a real person? Do you have someone dedicated to answering the phone, or does your front desk person have to juggle between checking people in, checking people out, and answering calls? Are there multiple people who answer the phone, or is it just one? If it's multiple, have they all been trained to answer the phone in the same way? And most importantly, do you ever miss calls?

When someone calls your practice, they're usually calling to book an appointment. If you don't answer the phone, what are they going to do next? Well, they'll probably call the next optometrist on Google. If they're a loyal patient, they might call back—but they might also get busy and forget.

Our average revenue per exam tends to be around $400, and most of the time when someone is calling our practice, it's to book an exam. Therefore, it's safe to say that every phone call is worth around $400. I need my team to know how important answering the phone is, so I've told them this. Every time they miss a phone call, it's like taking four $100 bills and tearing them up. Would you ever do that? Of course not. But that's exactly what's happening when you miss a phone call.

If we assume that $400 per phone call is reasonably close, we can do some simple math to figure out what this equates to over time. Two missed phone calls per week would be $800 in potentially lost revenue, which comes out to around $40,000 lost per year. $40,000 lost just from missing two phone calls per week! And I can tell you from experience that most practices are missing more than two calls per week.

What's the lesson here? Well, there are a few things to consider. The first is that, in this day and age, having a real person answer the phone actually sets you apart. So many businesses have phone trees or try to push people to book appointments online, and no one wants to do that. So if you don't have someone physically answering your phone, I would highly recommend considering it.

The other thing to consider is whether you have one person dedicated to answering the phone or not. It might sound crazy to hire someone *just to answer the phone,* but look at the numbers we just went over. If you miss even a few phone calls per week, that could be the equivalent of a full-time employee in lost revenue. Your practice should be set up so that someone is always able to answer the phone, even when patients are checking in and out or asking questions at the front desk.

So, how do you achieve that? The answer is simple. *Don't make your front desk person answer the phone!* In fact, they should be the *last* person to answer the phone! Their job is to interact with every single person that comes in your door, and they can't do that if they're on the phone all the time.

I have a story about this that really solidified my thinking, and I think it's pretty funny, so I'll tell you the whole thing. I've always said that you should tailor your practice to the 25 to 60-year-old female because they make all the decisions. How do I know this is true? Well, a few times per month, I will walk into the exam room and there will be a guy sitting there thinking he'd rather be anywhere else but here. I'll greet him and say, "What brought you to see us today?" You can probably guess what he says next. "Well, my wife thought I should have an eye exam." Sound familiar?

I've been doing this for 30 years. I am still waiting for the day I walk into an exam room and a woman says, "My husband thought I should have an eye exam." It hasn't happened once, and I don't think it ever will. In fact, if this does happen to you, I'd love to hear about it. Shoot me an email!

Anyway, one day I found myself at a bar in the Atlanta airport with seven women next to me, all between the ages of 25 and 60. We're stranded at the airport, so I started talking to them. I saw this as a chance to get some feedback from my exact target audience. I asked them one simple question: *What do you hate about going to the eye doctor or a doctor in general?*

Now, this is a study of n = 7, so it's not exactly statistically significant, but the first thing they all said was, "I don't want to walk into the doctor's office and the first thing I see is someone holding their finger telling me to wait because they're on the phone."

That is why I don't recommend having your front desk person answer the phone. You want your patients to feel welcomed and important when they come into your office. You also want to make sure your phone is answered promptly and at all times. *Those two things do not go together.* If you want both, you need to separate those responsibilities.

Yet the vast majority of practices I visit have their front desk person answering the phone! I actually did a talk to a group of optometrists the other night, and I surveyed the audience. I asked who answered their phone, and 70% of them said their front desk person. That is absolutely, positively the *last* person that should be answering the phone in your practice.

The lesson is that you should have one person whose sole job is to answer the phone. Ideally, they would be in a separate room or even off-site. There are plenty of companies that you can outsource this to, although you'll need to spend a few months training them. I typically recommend hiring for this, and it's probably the most common recommendation I make at all the practices I visit. If your front desk person is answering the phone, you are probably leaving money on the table and you may even be providing a subpar experience for your patients.

Now, one of the last things to consider is tracking your missed phone calls. This sounds simple—and it can be—but one problem is that employees might not want to admit when they've missed a phone call. If you've followed the advice from Chapters 1 and 2, that shouldn't be a problem. Just explaining the whole situation to your team and letting them know they're not going to get in trouble for missing a phone call, but you do want them to track it, would be a good start. There are also phone systems that will track this information (such as Weave) for you, along with your conversion rates (the percentage of phone calls that result in a booked appointment).

I can't understate how important it is to make sure you are not missing phone calls. And once you've got that figured out, you'll want to think about *how* your team handles those phone calls…

How You Answer the Phone

While we're on the topic of phone calls, I'd like to take a minute to explain how my team answers the phone. Because the truth is, picking up the phone is only half the battle—*how* you answer the phone makes a big difference.

I learned a great phone technique from a practice that I coached a while back. They had a woman who was absolutely incredible on the phone, and nearly every person who called ended up booking an appointment. So I sat down next to her and just listened to how she answered a few phone calls. Here's what she did.

No matter what the caller said, she always started the same way: "Thank you for calling! Have you ever been here before?"

If they said yes: "Great! We love when our patients come back. *When were you thinking of coming in?*"

If they said no: "What seems to be the problem?" And then after they explained, she'd say, "Our doctors are great at that! *When were you thinking of coming in?*"

Notice the pattern? She always ended with scheduling. Not "Would you like to schedule an appointment?" or "Can I help you with anything else?" It was always, *"When were you thinking of coming in?"*

It was absolutely genius. That question is so innocuous and disarming, it's almost impossible not to answer. The key is that you're not actually asking them to commit to anything, so answering is easy. Imagine if you were on the other side of that phone call. Even if you weren't ready to make an appointment yet, you'd probably say something like: "Well, probably next week, but I want to ask some questions first…" You haven't committed to an appointment, but you're already thinking about coming in, and you've given her some vital information.

Her response to that might be something like: "We can absolutely get your questions answered, and just so you know, we have open slots on Wednesday, Thursday, and Friday. Would any of those work for you?" Once again, it would almost be harder *not to* give her an answer!

I loved that system, and as soon as I came back to my practice, I went to our phone operator and told them I wanted to try out that exact script. It has made a huge difference in our conversion rates. What I learned from this was that if someone is calling you, they are already expressing interest in coming in. They already know the answer to that question—"When were you thinking of coming in?"—so if you ask them that right away, they're probably going to tell you. The answer to that makes the rest of the conversation a whole lot smoother.

Answering the phone does not have to be complicated. Really, all you need to do is have a dedicated person answering the phone who has been trained on a simple script. You need to have a strategy for your phone calls; you can't just leave it up to chance. If you're not doing this already, I guarantee you will see results with just a few quick changes.

2. No-Shows, Cancellations, Late Patients, and Empty Slots

This is another very common silent killer, and it's similar to missed phone calls in that you are simply losing revenue every time it happens. Every time a patient no-shows, cancels, or you have an empty slot in your schedule, you are losing revenue. If you're not actively working to prevent these things from happening, you're leaving money on the table.

The reality is that you should be seeing 90% of your possible appointments. That means if you have 100 appointment slots available in a week, you should be filling at least 90 of them with patients who actually show up. If you're falling short of that number, you've got work to do.

No-shows are one of the most common occurrences, and they're something that many doctors feel they have no control over. After all, you can't go out and make someone come into your office. But you can control what happens next.

If you are experiencing a lot of no-shows, my advice would be to start by looking at what you're doing to prevent them from happening in the first place. Are you sending reminder calls or texts? This might sound obvious, but a lot of practices skip this. We send out reminders 48 hours before each appointment, and that has helped a lot with no-shows. It ensures people don't forget and sometimes it might actually result in a cancellation because they realize something came up and they won't be able to make it anymore.

If that's the case, then we now have an empty slot on our calendar (another silent killer). This is not necessarily bad. When we book appointments, we keep a list of people who want to get in sooner. As soon as we have a cancellation, we call everyone on that list and let them know a slot has opened up. Nine times out of ten, that slot will be filled within an hour or two. And because we send out 48-hour reminders, we can often fill those slots even when people cancel at the "last minute."

Another thing to consider with no-shows is *when* they're happening. Is it a specific day of the week? A specific time of day? In my experience, no-shows tend to be worse on certain days and at certain times. Once you know when the problem is worst, you can start implementing systems to fix it. For example, in our practice, we realized that no-shows were most common right after lunch. We take lunch from 12:30 to 1:30, so we decided to reserve a 30-minute window for walk-ins and "optical emergencies" from 1:30 to 2:00 on Mondays and Thursdays.

Now, when we make the "is everything okay?" phone call after a no-show, we'll say something like:

"Hey, we noticed that you're having a hard time coming in for your appointments. That's no problem, we know you're busy and things happen. We just wanted to let you know that we are open for walk-ins between 1:30 and 2:00 every Monday and Thursday now, and we'd love to see you on one of those days."

We don't even give them the option to book an appointment because we know they're probably going to cancel, but we'd still love to see them. If they can come in during those windows, great! If not, it's no big deal.

If you have an admin day or some slow times in your week, this might be a good option for you. Make those times for walk-ins only, and tell your no-shows they can come in during those times. Best case scenario, you make a little extra money. Worst case scenario, you spend some time working on your business.

Now, what about late patients? One thing I'll say right off the bat is that if your goal is to give your patients the best possible care, it is not in your best interest to charge them late fees or get angry at them if they're late. Things happen. People aren't perfect. That's why the first thing we do when someone is late to an appointment is to ask them if everything is okay.

It's amazing how often the answer is no. "No, I had a flat tire." "No, I got into a car accident—it was a total nightmare." "No, my son had an emergency and I had to pick him up from school." When you hear these answers, it puts things into perspective. The last thing I want to do to these people is charge them a fee or make their day worse by telling them they can't see me. We truly care about our patients. When we ask if everything is okay, it's genuine.

After that first question, we then have a simple system. Our front desk person will say, "I'm so sorry that happened to you. Dr. Steele is already into his next patients—you're welcome to stay here, and he'll get to you as soon as he can, but it might take a little while. Or his last patient is at 4:00, you're welcome to come back at 4:30 and he can see you then, or we can reschedule you."

We give them three choices, and one of those choices involves me staying a little bit later than I normally would. That is totally fine with me—I am willing to do that for my patients if it will help them out. If my team needs to leave at five, I am cross-trained in all their roles and I am more than happy to take care of the patient entirely on my own. Remember, team first!

The key here is to have a system. You can't control whether patients show up or not, but you can create systems to incentivize them to show up and lower the risk of no-shows, cancellations, and empty slots.

3. Accounts Receivable

I know I said the first two were big ones, but accounts receivable (A/R) really is another big one. This actually might be the silent killer that costs practices the most money, and it's another one that many doctors feel they don't have control over. If you're not managing your A/R aggressively, you're basically giving patients (and insurance companies) an interest-free loan. And trust me, that adds up fast.

Banks also care about this. In fact, they have a system for this, which you should be aware of (because it's pretty accurate). They want less than 10% of your A/R to be over 90 days old, and the other 90% should be less than 30 days old. Here's why. In their eyes, any debts older than 90 days are essentially worthless. They just assume that you're never going to collect it because statistically speaking, you're probably not. Your chances of getting that money are so low that you can basically consider it gone.

Similarly, for debts between 31 and 60 days old, they assume a 50% collection rate. And for debts between 61 and 90 days old, they assume a 10% collection rate. These are generally good rules of thumb to follow, but the lesson is obvious: *don't let your A/R get past 30 days!* If your numbers are outside this range, that's a problem that could be costing you tens of thousands of dollars.

One of the biggest culprits here is **not collecting copays or deductibles upfront.** This is huge. If you're not collecting copays and deductibles at the time of service, you're creating unnecessary work for yourself and leaving money on the table. Patients are way more likely to pay when they're standing right in front of you than they are to mail in a check three weeks later, or pay online, or pay over the phone.

The bottom line is that your A/R should be one of your top priorities. I'd suggest reviewing it monthly or even weekly, if you're not already.

4. Spiffs and Freebies

If you're "too nice" (like me, apparently) this might be a big one for you. For what it's worth, I do find most optometrists are nice people and like giving things away to friends and family or offering steep discounts (or at least feel obligated to). At the end of the day, this really comes down to your own personal preference and how much you're willing to give away, but the reality is that it can add up quickly—like you saw in the beginning of this chapter.

When I talk about spiffs, what I'm really referring to is **freebies for family and friends.** Regardless of what you want to do here, you need a *written policy* around it. You can't just be giving stuff away willy-nilly. You need to be able to draw the line somewhere.

For example, maybe you give a 50% discount to family, staff, and family of staff. But what happens when your employee's cousin needs new contacts? Do they get the discount? What about their grandmother who has glaucoma? Where do you draw the line? If you don't have rules in place, these conversations can get awkward and many doctors feel obligated to give discounts to people who really don't fall within the "family" category. I hate to say it, but people do tend to take advantage of these discounts—and if you're too nice, you can fall victim to it.

My advice is to start by creating a written policy for friends and family discounts or freebies. Decide what you're comfortable with—maybe staff get products at cost, a 50% discount, or one free annual exam for immediate family. Whatever you decide is fine, but it needs to be written down and communicated to everyone. When you run into those awkward situations in the future where the line isn't totally clear, make a call and update your policy accordingly. I can't tell you how nice this is once you have it in place—not only will it save you money, but when someone asks for a discount all you have to do is point them to the policy. No more awkward conversations.

Removing Silent Killers From Your Practice

In previous chapters, I talked about how metrics are meaningless unless you actually do something about them, or use them as tools in your business. I'll give you the same advice here—knowing about these silent killers is one thing, but it's not going to change anything in your business. The whole point of identifying these problems is to implement systems to fix them.

So, here's my challenge for you: Pick one of these silent killers and focus on fixing it over the next 30 days. Maybe it's implementing a better phone system so you don't miss calls. Maybe it's cracking down on no-shows with reminder texts and a stricter policy. Maybe it's finally getting your A/R under control.

Whatever it is, take action and implement a system to manage it. You might be surprised at how quickly you can get a handle on some of these things. Heck, you could write down a spiff policy in a few minutes! But if you don't do anything, I can promise you these problems won't fix themselves.

In the next chapter, we're going to (finally) discuss how to talk to patients, or as I like to call it, how to NOT sell to patients. This is one of the most important parts of optometry and one that so many people get wrong—because they never received the right training.

This is the chapter I've been asked the most to write about, and you might be wondering why I've left it until the end. Here's the way I look at it. If you're building a house, you need to start with the foundation. I would consider the content we've discussed up to this point—team culture, leadership, metrics, the silent killers—to be foundational knowledge. You *need* to have that knowledge if you want to grow your practice.

Knowing how to talk to patients is great, but if your team isn't performing well, if you have high turnover, if you aren't tracking any metrics, or if there are silent killers draining thousands of dollars from your business every week, you stand to gain far more from fixing those problems than improving the way you talk to patients.

So, now that we've gotten all that covered, let's move on to the fun stuff.

Key Takeaways

1. **Silent killers are likely costing you money right now without your awareness.** If you're not actively measuring and managing things like missed phone calls, no-shows, poor A/R management, and spiffs, they could be costing your practice thousands or even tens of thousands of dollars per year. You won't notice the impact until you start tracking them, but once you do, you might be shocked at how much they add up.

2. **Every missed phone call is money out the window.** You should be answering at least 90% of your calls. If your phone is currently being answered by your front desk person, you may want to consider hiring a phone operator or outsourcing this—it's that important. Ideally, you'll also have a system for tracking missed calls and conversion rates.

3. **These problems won't solve themselves.** Knowing about them isn't enough, you have to implement systems to fix these problems. Pick one silent killer and commit to fixing it over the next 30 days. Spiffs are an easy way to start—write down your spiff policy and send it to your team to ensure everyone is on the same page. You could do that in five minutes!

Part 3
Patients

8.

How to NOT Sell to Patients

There's a dirty little secret in optometry that nobody likes to talk about, but I'm just going to come right out and say it:

Part of our job does involve *selling*.

There, I said it!

Now, I know that is an uncomfortable word—trust me, I hate it too—and no optometrist wants to think of themselves as a salesperson. But the reality is that your patients are paying money for glasses and contact lenses. These products generate revenue for your practice, and are a win-win for both you and the patient. They are going to see better and you are going to be more profitable.

But here's the thing: you are not a salesperson and you do not have to push products on your patients (nor should you). You also don't need to learn sleazy sales tactics or talk to patients like a used car salesman. That would only hurt your practice. ***All you need to do is focus on providing the best care for your patients***.

In this chapter, we're going to talk about how to *not* sell in the exam room. While part of your job does involve recommending products, I don't want you to think of yourself as a salesperson. That's why, throughout this chapter, I'm going to replace the word "selling" with "*not* selling"—because you are not selling to your patients, you are prescribing what's best for their ocular health. We will be focusing on how to have normal (not awkward!) conversations with your patients that help you give them the best care possible while increasing your revenue per exam in the process.

To put it another way, what if you could walk into the exam room and talk to each patient as if they were one of your close friends? What if you could recommend something to them and know that, more often than not, they'll buy it simply because they trust you? And what if, in doing that, you were able to provide even better care for your patients and help them improve their eye health? That is all possible, it's easier than you think, and you will be ready to make it happen by the end of this chapter.

Transformational, Not Transactional

If there is one overarching lesson you take from this entire chapter, it would be to focus on building transformational relationships—not transactional ones. There is a huge difference between the two.

A transactional relationship is when I walk into the exam room and say, "Okay, you need this $600 pair of glasses." That's it. They pay, leave, and maybe they come back next year, or maybe they don't. Or maybe they don't pay at all, and they just go buy some cheap glasses online because they don't want to pay $600 for glasses. Either way, the conversation is focused on the product and the price. I'm just trying to sell you the most expensive pair of glasses to maximize my profit.

A transformational relationship is completely different. This is when I'm doing what's best for my patients' eye health and vision, and they're trusting me to do it. My team and I have run all the tests, I've asked a number of questions to understand the patient's needs, and I'm making a recommendation based on all that information and my own expertise. I'm not just telling them to buy a $600 pair of glasses, I'm telling them exactly why that $600 pair of glasses will help their vision and why it's necessary over the cheaper options. Or maybe I'm even telling them that the $600 option isn't worth it for their situation, and they'll be fine with a less expensive lens.

The difference is that I am focused on transforming their eye health for the better, and I'm making that abundantly clear to them from the get-go. I'm building trust and developing real relationships with our patients, not because I want to make money off them, but because I genuinely care about them and want to do what's best for their health.

When patients trust you and believe you have their best interests at heart, they'll drive 40 minutes to see you even when there are plenty of other eye clinics in their town. They'll take off work early to make their appointment rather than coming in because you happen to be the only place open at 7:00 PM. That's a transformational relationship, and that's what this entire book has been building toward.

The best part is that when you focus on building transformational relationships, you don't have to worry about the "selling" part. You don't have to sell anything—the transaction happens naturally because you're doing what's legitimately best for them.

Throughout this chapter, I'm going to show you how to have conversations that build these transformational relationships. These aren't sales techniques—they're communication strategies that help you educate patients, understand their needs, and make recommendations they can trust. And the first one involves one simple word.

Start With Why

Years ago, I watched a TED Talk that completely changed the way I talk to our patients. It's called *Start With Why: How Great*

Leaders Inspire Action, by Simon Sinek. If you haven't seen it, I would highly recommend watching it on YouTube.

In the video, Sinek talks about how successful companies like Apple and even people like Martin Luther King and the Wright Brothers were able to succeed when so many others didn't. I'm not going to go into all the details because, frankly, he does a much better job of explaining it than I would. What I will tell you is that those companies and people were successful because they understood the value of explaining *why.* Apple didn't just tell people they had great computers; they started with *why* they were building great computers and why their products would help their customers.

See, most people don't make decisions based on information alone—they need to know *why.* I am not a neuroscientist, so if you want to know all the details about how this works, I'd suggest watching the video. But the gist is that when you start with "why," you are talking directly to the part of the brain that controls behavior. When you follow that up with information, decisions become straightforward. If you approach it the other way around or you leave out the "why," it doesn't work nearly as well.

Have you ever been presented with a bunch of information about a large purchase—technical specs, white papers, and whatnot—but something still just didn't feel right? I'd bet you didn't make that purchase. That's because you didn't understand the *why,* even though you clearly understood the what and the how.

Conversely, I'll bet you've made plenty of purchases because they just felt "right," even without all the information. That's probably because you understood the "why." I had one of those situations recently, and it was actually pretty funny. I was driving down the interstate in Virginia, on my way to a speaking engagement, listening to the radio, when someone came on and said, "Do you want to spend more time with your wife and play more golf, or do you want to keep mowing your yard and cleaning your house?"

I don't even mow my own lawn, but still I immediately thought, "Yes! I want all of those things!" I actually started pulling over on the highway, hoping I could find a pen and paper in this rental car to write down whatever this place was. It turned out to be a commercial for a retirement home! I have no plans to retire any time soon, but they got me by starting with "why," not what they did.

So, what does this mean for you? If you want to get better at talking to patients, if you want to build better relationships with them, and if you want to increase your revenue per exam, the golden rule is to *start with why.* Tell patients *why* you're doing something before you do it.

This might sound obvious, but most doctors don't do this. They just walk in and start asking questions or doing tests without any context. Maybe they're just busy, or they're just going through the motions. That might be okay if your patient is a robot, but our patients are human beings. And human beings want to know why things are happening, especially when it comes to their own health.

Here's what this looks like in my practice. I should add that my editors originally wanted me to trim this down, but I told them no because I want you to see exactly how this works. When I walk into the exam room with a new patient, the conversation goes something like this:

"Hi there [patient first name], I appreciate you coming in today. Now, some people insist on calling us doctor, so if you want to call me Doctor Steele, you can. My friends call me Kurt, and you're more than welcome to call me Kurt. Some people like to use Doc, and that's fine too.

Now, I'm going to start by asking you some questions about where you work and what you like to do in your spare time. And there's a reason for that. When it comes to glasses, there is no such thing as a perfect prescription. And what I mean by that is there are several lenses I can show you that you'll be able to see those letters with. There's not just one. You have a range of vision, and I can move that out and I can move that in.

In other words, I wouldn't prescribe a bank teller like I would a truck driver. I might get the same numbers, but there's a big difference between staring at a computer screen eight hours a day and driving a truck for a living. Those are two completely different visual needs. Even if I get the same numbers, I'll probably prescribe two different things.

So I need to ask you these questions, because I want to make sure I get your vision where you need it to be. I want to protect your eye health and make sure we use the right technology to do that, whatever that is. How does that sound?"

I've actually had people tell me they came back to my practice just because I said that. They told me they liked knowing that I'm prioritizing their vision. That just shows you how much of a difference starting with "why" can make.

I could have just walked in and started asking them questions, but if I did that, they'd be sitting there wondering, "Why is he asking me all of this?" or "Why does he care so much about my personal life?" They might not even want to give me honest answers if they think I'm just prying for no reason. But when they understand the *why,* they actually *want* to answer my questions because they know it will help their vision. They also immediately trust me because they know I'm prioritizing their ocular health.

This is actually something I've trained my entire team to do. My team doesn't just start doing tests on our patients; they explain why they're doing them. So they might come in and say, "Hi there, we're doing this test because we want to make sure you don't have glaucoma." Even my front desk people know to start with why. They won't just say, "Can I have your insurance card?" They might say, "I'd like to take a look at your insurance card so I can make sure you're getting as much of this covered as possible."

Best vs. Right

For a long time, I used to tell our patients that I was going to recommend the "best" technology for their ocular health. You may have noticed from that previous excerpt that I now say the "right" technology instead. I made that shift because I started to notice that patients would get worried when I said the "best" technology, because that's typically the most expensive. Most of the time, people don't want the absolute best—they want what's right for them.

So, now I use the word "right" because it means they're going to get the best value. I'm not going to prescribe the most expensive thing because it will make me the most money; I'm going to prescribe the *right* thing, whatever that is. If it happens to be expensive, so be it. If not, that's fine too. Really, it's in my best interest to give the patient what they need and not oversell them on anything. If I just tried to sell the most expensive products to every patient, a lot of people would just say no and never come back. Or maybe they'd feel pressured into saying yes, but then they'd tell their friends about how expensive I was and likely find another doctor.

Either way, it's better for me and the patient to just prescribe what's *right* for them rather than trying to make a quick buck.

Educating Patients

Another way to think about this "why" concept is to focus on educating your patients. Patients love learning, so rather than just telling them what you're doing, teach them something about their eyes or why certain things matter. When you educate them, you're showing them that you care about more than just selling them something. Plus, most people find eyes to be fascinating. (Because they are fascinating!)

So, rather than just telling the patient that you're taking a photo of the back of their eye, maybe start by asking them if they know what the macula is. If not, you could give them a quick run-down so they understand why the photo is important and even why they should be getting an eye exam every year:

> *"We are going to take a high definition photo of the back of your eye. It helps the doctor make sure there isn't any*

retinal disease. We can save this, and it's like having a photo album of the back of your eye as time goes on. How does that sound?"

Imagine being a patient and hearing that, versus "Look straight ahead into the camera... Okay, all done," with no context. I'm sure you can see the difference that a little education makes. It's more enjoyable for the patient, it illustrates "why," it builds trust, and it only takes a minute or two. And hey, a quick conversation like that could even inspire someone to become an optometrist one day!

The overarching lesson I'd like you to take from this is that starting "why" doesn't have to be some formula, and you certainly don't need to follow my script. Just remember to always explain *why* you're doing something and *why* you're recommending something. Use the word "because" if you can, and try to educate your patients in the process! That alone will make a big difference in the conversations you're having with patients, and it should feel very natural.

Asking Questions

Okay, now we're going to move into some of the more specific verbiage I like to use when talking with patients. Most of these are simple, and some of them I just picked up through life—they don't even have anything to do with optometry! That's because a lot of this boils down to treating people well and building real relationships with them. Remember in Chapter 2 when I said you should be friends with your team? Well, the same concept applies here—being friendly with your patients will get you far.

The first of these tips is to ask questions, and this is something I picked up from my Dad. He had this saying: "He who is asking the questions is in charge of the conversation." I learned that from him, and it's stuck with me ever since.

This is one of those tips that applies to both optometry and life. Asking questions gives you control over the conversation and helps you gather information. But most importantly, it shows the other person that you care about them.

I was on a plane once, and practically everyone on the plane seemed to know the woman sitting next to me. So, I asked her why she was so popular. It turns out she was a famous actor from a television show. Now, I know very little about acting, and I didn't know much about the show she was on, but I was curious, so I just kept asking her questions. "What other shows have you been in?" "How did you get into acting?" "What's your favorite role you've ever played?" "What's the most interesting project you've ever worked on?"

Before I knew it, we'd talked for the entire flight. And I'll never forget this—when we landed, she gave me her phone number and said, "You know, I loved talking to you because you treated me like a human being, not a celebrity." I had to laugh because all I did was ask questions and listen!

If you want to give your patients the best possible care, then you need to start by asking questions. How can you tell them what they need if you don't have any information? So one of the best things you can do is to start by asking questions and getting them talking. Find out what's bothering them, what their concerns are, and what their lifestyle is like. Answers to those questions alone will help you provide better care and show the patient that you are interested in helping them.

For example, I always ask our patients what they do for work. If they work in an office, I'll ask them if they're looking at a screen (or multiple screens) all day. If so, I'll ask them how their eyes feel at the end of the day. I also ask if the screen is above, below, or level with their line of sight. I'll ask them if they have any neck or shoulder pain. I might ask them how their monitor is positioned to see if they've got their desk set up right. From there, I can make some inferences about what they need. I might say something like, "Okay, because you said your neck and shoulders hurt at the end of the day, I'm going to recommend a second pair of glasses specifically for computer work that should help with that."

That's just one situation, but the concept applies to every patient. Ask questions to gain as much information as possible so you can give the best care possible.

Here are some other examples of great questions to ask:

For contact lenses:

- "When do your contact lenses begin to feel dry?"
- "On a scale of 1 to 10, how would you rank your current contact lenses?"
- "At what point in the month do you start to feel your contacts?"

For second pairs of glasses:

- "How do your eyes feel after being on the computer for eight hours?"
- "How do your neck and shoulders feel at the end of the day?"
- "What do you do when the sun is really bright?"

For Transitions lenses:

- "What do you do when you need sunglasses but you're already wearing your regular glasses?"
- "Do you find yourself squinting a lot when you go outside on bright days?"
- "How often do you find yourself switching between your glasses and sunglasses throughout the day?"

You'll notice that these are not yes-or-no questions. They're open-ended, which means patients have to actually think about their answer and give you real information. And once they start talking about their problems, you can then provide them with a solution.

The Word "Because"

Asking questions will give you the information you need to make a recommendation, but the way you word that recommendation is important. Earlier in this chapter, we talked about the value of starting with *why.* There is a simple way to do this that has multiple benefits, and it's to use the word "because." This has an almost magical power to make people agree with you—which might sound crazy, but it's true.

There's a famous study called the copier study, where researchers tested different ways of asking to cut in line at a copy machine. When the person said, "Can I cut in front of you and make these copies, because I'm really in a hurry?" 94% of people said yes. When they said, "Can I cut in front of you and make these copies?" 30% said yes. And when they said, "Can I cut in front of you to make these copies, because I really want to make these copies?" it went back up to 93%. He just repeated the same question, but threw the word *because* in there! You would think the first question worked because they were in a hurry, but this proves it was due to the word "because."

The word "because" triggers an automatic compliance response in our brains. When we hear that word, we assume there's a good reason behind the request, even if the reason doesn't actually make sense. Now, I'm not saying you should use meaningless reasons with your patients. What I am saying is that you should always, always, always give them a reason for what you're doing or recommending. And the best way to do that is to use the word "because."

Once you've asked some questions, this becomes incredibly easy. All you need to do is take the patient's pain point (which they've just told you) and put the word "because" in front of it, then give your recommendation. So if a patient tells me their eyes feel really tired after being on the computer all day, I'll say: "**Because** you said your eyes feel really tired after being on the computer all day, I'm recommending a pair of computer glasses."

For contact lenses, it might be: "**Because** you said your eyes dry out before the end of the day, I'm recommending daily contact lenses."

Or if they mention that the sun bothers them when they're driving, I'll say: "**Because** you said the sun really bothers you when you're driving, I'm recommending prescription sunglasses."

See how simple that is? I am literally using their own words in my recommendation. This accomplishes three things: First, it shows them that I was listening to what they said (which builds trust). Second, it gives them a specific reason for my recommendation that they can't really argue with because it came from their own mouth. And third, it uses that magic word "because."

It sounds simple—and it is—but it makes a massive difference. When patients understand why you're doing something, they trust you more. They feel like you're working with them instead of just doing stuff to them.

The Herd Theory

After I've made my recommendation using "because," I immediately follow it up with another science-backed strategy called the herd theory. This is where I let the patient know that they're not alone in this decision—that many of our other patients have made the same choice and they're happy with it.

Think about it this way. When was the last time you chose a restaurant based on its Yelp reviews? Or booked a hotel because of its rating? We all do this. We figure that if something works for most people, it will work for us. It makes perfect sense.

This phenomenon is called herd theory, or social proof. It's the idea that humans tend to adopt the behaviors or attitudes of the majority. There are plenty of examples of this, but one I love is an old video about social conformity from the show Candid Camera. There's a hidden camera in an elevator, and you can see one person inside the elevator, facing the door like normal. Then, a bunch of paid actors get into the elevator one by one, and they all stand facing away from the door. They don't say anything, they just stand there and wait for the elevator to start moving. The guy facing forward is looking around, confused, and within about thirty seconds, he turns around to face the same way as them. It's pretty funny, and I bet you'd do the same thing if you were in his shoes.

The lesson for us is that people like to make decisions based on what the majority does. They figure if it works for everyone else, it will probably work for them, which is true nine times out of ten.

One simple way to use this to your advantage is to just say "a lot of our patients do ______." And I shouldn't really say it like that because you're not taking advantage of anyone. Really, you're just telling them what most people do, which makes the decision easier for them. Here are those examples from earlier, now expanded with the herd theory:

- **For computer glasses:** "Because you said your head, neck, and shoulders really bother you at the end of a long day, I'm recommending computer glasses. A lot of our patients get these, and they love them. They say they see better, their eyes feel better, and I'm seeing fewer eye infections. How does that sound?"

- **For daily contact lenses:** "Because your eyes dry out before the end of the day, I'm recommending daily contact lenses. Most of our patients wear daily lenses, and they love them. They say they see better, their eyes feel better, and I'm seeing fewer eye infections."

- **For prescription sunglasses:** "Because you said the sun really bothers you when you're driving, I'm recommending prescription sunglasses. A lot of our patients get these, and they love them. They say they're more convenient than using clip-ons, and they're a lot better for your eye health and your safety than driving with the sun in your eyes."

I'm not telling them to buy something or claiming that this is the best solution; I'm just letting them know that other people have made this choice and they're happy with it. That can take a lot of pressure off the patient because it makes it feel like a sure bet. They can (rightly) assume that if it works for most people, it will work for them as well. Imagine if I said, "You know, not a lot of people choose this option, and I haven't heard anything great about it—but you're welcome to try it if you want." How quickly would you say no to that offer?

The Law of Diffusion of Innovation

There's another concept called the law of diffusion of innovation that is worth knowing about, as it will help you understand how some of your patients make decisions. This law explains how new technologies or products spread throughout a population, and it's backed by real science. Rather than go through all the scientific details, I'll give you my version as it applies to optometry. This is based on the law itself, but also what I've seen with my patients and those of my clients.

The law breaks people down into three categories: early adopters, the majority, and laggards. Generally speaking, you can assume that each one of your patients will fall into one of those three categories.

20% of people are early adopters. These are the type of people who want the latest technology regardless of price. They're the first ones to get a new iPhone, and they'll happily pay more for the latest, greatest thing. These people are not the norm, but they do exist. I'll tell you a quick story about one.

I once got talking to a guy on a plane, and when he found out I was an optometrist, he told me he wanted to find a new optometrist himself because he wasn't happy with his current one. Turns out I actually knew his current optometrist, and I knew he was a great doctor. So I asked him why he wanted to switch. He told me, "Well, I've been wearing these two-week lenses for eight or nine years. Every time I go in there, he asks me how my contacts are, and I say they're fine. Hasn't anything new come out?"

Now, this can be a teaching moment here. Any married man will tell you that when his wife says she's "fine," that's not really the case. I've also heard fine defined as an acronym: Feelings I'm Not Expressing! The point is, he was telling his doctor his contacts were fine, and the doctor took that to mean everything was okay—but he was about to find a new doctor! If his doctor had just asked a few more questions to find out what was really going on, he could've better understood his patient's needs, recommended a better lens, and kept the patient. This is why you always ask questions!

So I started asking my normal questions about his vision, how often he replaces his lenses, and what specific problems he was having. Turns out, he was a model patient—he had no problems, he took his lenses out every night, and he even replaced them every two weeks, which was shocking. So I told him, "Look, those contacts are perfectly fine for you. But if you really want something new and you really want to take the best possible care of your eyes, they have daily lenses now where you can just throw them away and get a clean lens every day."

He got all excited and said, "See? That's exactly what I'm talking about! I would do that in a heartbeat!" He didn't care that it was more expensive; he just wanted the latest, greatest technology. He was an early adopter, and although early adopters are not the norm, it's important to be aware that around 20% of your patients genuinely just want the best thing out there—and they're willing to pay for it. You can see how asking questions led me to discover that, and how I was able to suggest something that an early adopter would get excited about.

60% of people are in the majority. These are your typical patients. They're not early adopters, but they're not laggards either. They want what most people want—proven products at a fair price. They're not going to pay an arm and a leg for the latest, greatest thing, but they do want a good value.

Finally, 20% are laggards. These are the cautious ones who are skeptical of new things. They're probably just going to get the cheapest thing they can get. And that's fine! This doesn't mean they're bad people; they're just frugal. Ironically, these are often the people who have the most money—because they never spend any of it! It's not personal, it's just how they are. The best part about laggards is that they can often become your best referrals: "Dr. Steele is great! He knows what he's talking about and gave me a great deal. He didn't try to sell me anything."

What's the lesson here? The big one is, **don't let the laggards affect how you talk to the majority.** We all have a tendency to do this because the laggards are the ones who affect us the most. The people who say "no" stick with you. They might start making you second-guess yourself or lowering your recommendations because you don't want to get another "no." But now that you know what a laggard is, you'll be able to spot them in your practice. When they say no, you'll understand that it had nothing to do with the way you spoke to them—they're just a laggard! Chances are, nothing you say will sway them! You're far better off letting them make their own decision and focusing your attention on the majority.

The other critical lesson is that all the verbiage we just went over works best with the majority. Those are the people who will actually be affected by the way you talk to them. The early adopters just want the best thing, and the laggards want the cheapest thing. There's not much you can do there. But the majority want the best value—something that solves their problem, isn't overly expensive, and has a proven track record. You need to explain to them why your recommendation is right for them, and if you can do that, they'll say yes.

Base your strategy on the majority, and go into most of your conversations assuming the patient is in that 60%. If you tailor your approach to the cheapest 20%, you're going to lose that critical 60% in the middle who actually want to hear about better options—they just need you to explain the why and show them that other people are happy with their decision.

Always Be Closing

This is another one from my dad. He listened to me do exams all day once, and afterward he said, "Son, you do a great job right until the end, but you never close." And he was right. I've now seen the same thing with many of the optometrists I coach, where they do a great job talking with patients and making recommendations, but they can never seal the deal at the end of the exam.

I've heard many consultants say you should always use the words prescribe or recommend instead of suggest, as if that's going to make the difference. What my dad would say to those people is: "It doesn't matter whether you prescribe, recommend, or suggest—if you don't close, you literally accomplished nothing."

Really, the best way to think about this is that you should always be steering the direction toward a verbal confirmation. You start by asking them some questions, finding their pain points, making a recommendation, using the word because, backing it up with the herd theory, and then asking for a verbal confirmation. That is really the formula in a nutshell.

You may have noticed this already, but whenever I talk to a patient about something, I always end with a closing question, like:

- "How does that sound?"
- "Do you see how that would help you?"
- "Does that sound like it would benefit you?"
- "Sound cool?" (I learned that one from Dr. Reshma Amin!)

I ask those questions because they require a verbal confirmation—a yes or no. And these are all fairly innocuous questions. I'm not staring them in the face and saying, "Are you going to buy this from me or not?!" I'm just presenting them with my recommendation and asking what they think.

The most important part is that when the patient says yes, you shut up. Don't keep talking. Don't try to overdo it. Don't give them time to reconsider. Make your recommendation, ask your closing question, and then wait for them to respond. The silence might feel awkward, but just let them think and respond. When they say yes, you can move right along to what I call "the handoff."

The Handoff

The handoff is what happens right after you've closed a patient in the exam room. This is one of the more important parts of "not selling" because you've just gotten them to agree to what you've recommended, and now you're handing off the actual transaction to someone else.

Here's how I do it. When I walk the patient up to the optical area, I introduce them to my optical team—Stephanie, Erica, Chasity, and Julia. Then I say:

> *"Stephanie, [Patient] and I are good with a second pair of glasses for computer work. [Patient], Stephanie is going to make sure you get exactly what we talked about in the exam room."*

And that's it. I shut up. I don't add anything else. I've already recommended what is best for the patient, and they have agreed, so I don't need to keep talking. I'll thank them for coming in, say goodbye, and walk away. Done!

Once again, the language choices here are specific. For example, I used to say "we agreed to," but I realized that sounded more like a contract negotiation, so I changed it to "are good with," which is a little more casual.

The phrase "are good with" is also important—this is like a little code between me and my team. Stephanie knows that if I say "we are good with" that means the patient is in agreement. The patient said yes, and Stephanie doesn't have to do anything except execute on what we discussed.

"We talked about" is different. If I say that, Stephanie knows the patient didn't say yes. Maybe the patient's a laggard. Stephanie knows that she now needs to talk to the patient about my recommendation, and she's trained to use the same verbiage. She'll use the herd theory and talk about how most of our patients love whatever it is I'm recommending. If that doesn't work, the patient is probably a laggard, and she'll just go right to the value product.

That code is great because I can't just go to Stephanie and say, "Hey Stephanie, I haven't closed this guy yet—can you take a stab at it?" I also want to make it quick and easy for both her and the patient if they have already committed.

You're welcome to use that exact strategy yourself—I can tell you it works well. But really, the most important thing is that you develop a *system* for the handoff and you train your team on it. The key is to make sure the patient knows we are on their side and want to do what's best for them and their budget. We are helping them get exactly what they need—almost like a pharmacist filling a prescription. (Actually, that's pretty much exactly what's happening!) You just need to communicate what you're prescribing and the status of that prescription.

One last tip is that if there are savings or if insurance is involved, you'll definitely want to bring that up in the hand-off. As you probably know, contact lens companies often have rebates, and a patient might have a vision benefit through their insurance. So in that case, I might say, "Stephanie is going to make sure you get both your vision benefit and the rebate we talked about so you can save as much as possible on your contacts today."

This is probably one of the best systems I have implemented in my business. If you can get it right, it makes closing a breeze and you avoid any awkwardness. It just works!

The Art of Downselling

The reality is that sometimes patients will push back on price. Not everyone will, but a certain percentage of people just want the cheapest thing, or they want to know that they're getting the best possible deal. When that happens, you need to know how to handle it.

First, there's a simple rule to follow when it comes to (not) selling: wherever you start, you cannot go up. Really, this just means you should always start by recommending the *right* product for the patient's needs, even if it is expensive. I think too many doctors are afraid their patients will balk at the price, or maybe they've just heard too many "no's" in the past. Either way, they start by recommending the less expensive or middle-of-the-road option even when their patient would be better off with the high-end product. They're leaving money on the table for themselves, but they're also compromising the ocular health of the patient!

Always start with the *right* product for your patient. If they are concerned about the price, then you can at least go down to a less expensive option. Moving the other direction is much more difficult, if not impossible. And keep in mind that this isn't about making the most money, it is about recommending the right product for the patient that will get their vision to where it needs to be.

The thing is, if you've been starting with "why" and building trust throughout the exam, the patient shouldn't be surprised when you offer them something that might seem expensive. They will understand that you're recommending what's truly right for them, and they will see the value in spending money to take care of their eyes.

If they still balk at the price, you can acknowledge their concern by saying something like, "I understand completely. We all have budgets. I was just recommending what was right for your eye health and vision." When I do this, I like to pause. I give them about seven seconds of silence (seriously). Sometimes patients will reconsider in that moment and say, "Okay, well if that's what is right for me, then I'll go ahead and get it."

If they remain quiet or still seem hesitant, that's when you employ the art of downselling. The key here is to make sure the patient understands what they're getting is not quite as good as what you initially recommended, but it's still pretty good, and a lot of your patients do well with it. Here's an example of how I might handle that situation with contact lenses:

"Listen, I do have another contact lens option that's a really good value. Now, it's not quite as good as the one I originally recommended—you may feel them a little more at the end of the day—but a lot of our patients get these. They're still really healthy and comfortable, and they do really well with them. I'm sure you'll do well with them, too. How does that sound?"

The important thing is that you don't just say, "Okay, you can get this cheaper version." If you don't explain the difference between the recommendation and the other option, then it sounds like you were just trying to sell them something expensive for no reason. When you do this right, you're giving them permission to choose the more affordable option while still feeling confident about their decision.

"We do have other options as well as the ones we've presented. Now, they're not quite as good as the original recommendation, and you may have to take care of them

a little more. You also get a one-year warranty instead of a two-year warranty. But a lot of our patients get these glasses, they do real well with them, and we can stand behind them. How does that sound?"

Also, right now we are losing lots of sales to online competitors like Zenni as well as cheap competitors like Costco. I was at a retreat recently, and we came up with this verbiage to combat the question, "I just want my prescription so I can get them cheaper elsewhere." What we came up with is, "My cheapest option is certainly not as cheap as Costco. If you're just looking for cheap, then that's probably where you should go; however, a lot of our patients find that we do have a budget-conscious line here that is a much better value, and if anything goes wrong, we can stand behind them. How does that sound?"

As someone who works in a poor, rural area, I have plenty of experience with this. While I want what's best for my patients, I would never try to push expensive products that they can't afford because I understand that money can be a significant barrier. I want what's best for them, and that includes what's best for their checkbook.

"I Just Want What My Insurance Covers"

Last but not least, it's time to cover the question every doctor dreads. "I just want what my insurance covers."

Now, to be fair, this is a very legitimate concern for many people. They might not be able to afford expensive products and they may have a vision benefit through their health insurance. It makes perfect sense that they would want to use that up and avoid paying out of pocket. Frankly, you would too if you were in their situation.

That said, it can be a challenging situation for doctors. It also tends to turn the conversation into a negotiation, which is not fun for anyone. So, let's talk about how to deal with this.

Remember: "He who is asking the questions is in charge of the conversation." Whenever a patient says they just want what their insurance covers, I'll respond with a question back. I'll actually grab their chart and flip through it, then say, "Okay, I see you have this vision plan and you want to make sure you're getting the most out of it. Do you mind me asking what your insurance covers?"

The number one answer I receive—and it's not even close—is "I don't know."

The second most common answer is "Doesn't it cover everything?"

I find this a bit puzzling. Think about what they're saying. They want what their insurance covers, but they don't know what their insurance actually covers. Imagine if I said, "Well, it looks like your insurance only covers half a pair of glasses, so here's one lens and half a frame. Have a good day!" It really makes no sense. It's like walking into a store with a gift card and saying, "I'll take whatever this gives me," without knowing how much is on the card or what the store even sells.

But here's the thing. As silly as this sounds to us, this is a very real concern for a lot of people, and it is our job as the doctor to find a solution that works for them and makes the most out of their vision benefit. When patients say they just want what their insurance covers, what they're really saying is: **"Hey, I like you and I'm trusting my eye care to you, but I only see you for about 30 minutes every year. Don't rip me off."** That's all it is. They want to get the full value from their insurance, and they don't want to be taken advantage of. That is totally normal.

Now, the verbiage we've discussed in this chapter and throughout the book should go a long way toward preventing this question in the first place. When patients like and trust you, they will know you're not ripping them off, so they won't default to "whatever my insurance covers." That said, this is still a common question even in my practice—here's how I handle it.

Whether they say "I don't know" or "Doesn't it cover everything?" my answer is the same. I say something along the lines of:

"Well, actually, your vision plan is pretty good and it covers a decent pair of glasses. Now, what a lot of our patients do is take this benefit and use it to get the best pair of glasses

at less than half the cost. You can get the glare coating, the nice frame, the nice lens, and you'll see much better. You'll get a better warranty, you'll enjoy them more, and you'll get every dime of that vision benefit. How does that sound?"

I'm letting them know that I am on their side. I'm not just working with their insurance plan, I'm helping them get the best possible value out of their benefit—*and critically,* I'm doing what's best for their eye health. Plus, I'm using the herd theory to let them know this is what most people do.

The insurance question is common, and it's totally valid. The thing is, when someone asks that question, it doesn't mean you can't make any money. It just means they want to know they're getting the most value out of their benefit, and you can easily work with them to make that happen. The best part is that as you implement the other techniques we've discussed, you should be getting this question less and less.

Going the Extra Mile

Throughout this book, I've talked a lot about systems, metrics, and data-driven decision-making. Those things are absolutely critical to building a successful practice. But there's another element that's just as important, even if it's harder to measure: going the extra mile for your patients.

My dad taught me this lesson better than anyone. Back in the mid-2000s, my dad decided to open his own metal roofing business after years of helping other companies turn around. The timing couldn't have been worse—he opened right before the 2008 financial crisis. The real estate market tanked, the economy collapsed, and my dad found himself in the worst financial situation of his life.

Around that same time, I was helping with a golf tournament for a local children's home. This wasn't just any charity— they took in kids that even foster parents wouldn't take and put them in a faith-based environment. They did incredible work turning lives around.

At the end of the tournament, there was a silent auction. And despite the fact that my dad was struggling financially, I watched him spend over $10,000 at that auction.

I knew what he was going through financially, and I told him he didn't have to spend that much. He looked at me and he said, "Son, those kids need that money way more than I do. And if you do it for the right reasons, God will give it back to you." I swear I felt the hair on the back of my neck stand up. Ever since then, I have always chosen to be generous wherever I can. My dad used to say that "you can't outgive God," and I now say it too. I believe it to be true. I truly believe that's part of why I've been so successful—not because I'm smarter than other optometrists, but because I've tried to be generous and go the extra mile for my patients.

Going the extra mile means looking out for the people you care about and finding ways to help them that they didn't even know existed. For example, I'll give my cell phone number to long-term patients and emergency cases. They don't have to ask for it; I just give it to them because I want them to know I've got their back. Yes, I get some calls at inconvenient times—but it's the right thing to do.

I have a patient with Parkinson's who has trouble putting his contact lenses in. So I put him on weekly lenses, and once a week, he comes into our office and I change his contacts for him. It takes five minutes, but it means everything to him.

I can remember one time when a patient's son passed away. She was one of my first patients ever, and when her son passed away, I knew what that level of grief was like. Losing my brother was one of the worst things that ever happened in my life, but the worst part about it was watching what it did to my mom. That is a level of grief that only a parent can understand.

When I went to the funeral, I brought an annual supply of contacts and just laid them on a chair in the front row. I went up to her, gave her a hug, and told her how sorry I was, and then I just said, "You're not even thinking about this now, and you don't have to worry about it. Your eyes are fine. I put an annual supply of contacts over there so you don't have to think about it, and I'll just see you next year." She was absolutely floored by that. The next time I saw her, she cried and told me I had no idea how much that meant to her.

I also had another patient who lost her business due to Hurricane Helene, and I did the same thing—I shipped her an annual supply of contacts and told her she had a lot more things to worry about than contacts, and I'll just see her in a year. When she opened back up, and my wife and I went to the opening night, she hugged my neck, cried, and told me that I had no idea how much that meant to her. It really gave her faith in humanity.

I don't do things like this to be some kind of hero. I do them because they're the right thing to do. If you're generous with your patients, if you go the extra mile, if you do the right thing even when it costs you something, it will come back to you in one way or another.

A Good Ol' Country Doctor

While the specific verbiage and strategies I've outlined here can be incredibly helpful, the big mindset shift I want you to walk away from this chapter with is to move from transactional relationships to transformational relationships.

This is not about learning sales techniques or manipulating people into buying stuff they don't need. It's about building a transformational relationship with each of your patients. How does that happen? Well, it ultimately has to start from a place of genuine care. If you really care about your patients and you want to do the right thing, it will all work itself out in the end.

I'd like to leave you with one last thought. My senior practice partner, Dr. Foster, used to have an amazing revenue per exam metric. Whenever I asked him his secret, he would say: *"I just talk to patients like a good ol' country doctor. When they come into the exam room, I act like they are coming to my house. This isn't an eye exam, it's a home visit."*

I saw the way that man conducted his exams, and that really was his approach. I never heard him say, "Have a seat," for example. He would always say, "Make yourself comfortable." He literally acted like they were coming to his house for a visit. And he must have been doing something right, because his patients would follow his recommendations.

I have taken this to heart, and it's something that can't be taught with a script or a framework. If you really want to develop better relationships with your patients, get to know them. Ask about their lives, their work, and their hobbies. Joke around with them. Be yourself! Be patient. Listen to them. Ask questions. *Care for them.* And then use that knowledge to make recommendations that will get their vision to where it needs to be.

I treat our patients like I would treat a friend, and guess what? Many of them *are* now friends of mine. I am friends with our patients, just like I'm friends with my team. How great is that? I get to work with people I love every day. My mom used to say, "The best thing you can be in life is a best friend," and I wholeheartedly agree.

When you put patients first and prioritize their eye health above profit, you create loyalty that money can't buy. Those patients will drive past other optometrists to see you. They'll refer their friends and family. They'll trust you with their vision, which is not something to be taken lightly. And most importantly, they'll stick around—not just because you're the best deal in town, but because they know, like, and trust you.

Conclusion & Action Plan

When I started writing this book, I kept thinking about that picture on my desk—the one from Green Bay with my brother Jason, Dr. Foster, my dad, and me. Four guys who loved football, loved life, and were just trying to enjoy a cold day watching the Packers. Three of them are gone now, and I'm the only one left in that picture.

Losing those three guys in such a short time taught me the most important business lesson I've ever learned. And it's a lesson I hope you'll take to heart, whether you remember anything else from this book or not: **Life is too short to spend it at a job you hate, working with people you don't like, doing things that don't matter.**

When I look back at my career, I spent way too many years grinding away, staying open late, working weekends, and basically running myself into the ground all in the name of putting patients first and growing the practice. I wasn't miserable, but I was operating under the philosophy that working long hours and doing everything myself was the only way to be successful. I was tired. My team was tired. We were surviving, but we weren't thriving.

When I look back at our growth, I can really boil it down to three key things:

1. Putting my team first
2. Using metrics to make smarter decisions
3. Building real relationships with our patients

The more I focused on those three things, the more we grew and the easier work became. We experienced exponential growth while cutting our hours and spending more time with our families. We started having fun at work. Team members stopped leaving. And our patients started driving past other optometrists just to see us.

The best part isn't the money, it's that I now love going to work. I love the people I work with. And I hope the people I work with feel like they *get* to come to work, not that they *have* to come to work. I take vacations and I don't feel guilty about it. When my team members take a vacation, I am genuinely thrilled for them—not frustrated that we'll have to cover for them. I work three days a week, and I'm making more money than I ever did when I was grinding five to six days per week, working evenings and weekends.

If you've gotten this far, you know this wasn't a matter of luck. It wasn't because I'm smarter than you or because I have some special advantage. It's because I finally learned to run my practice like a business. I learned how to be a real leader, track my metrics, and talk to patients like a doctor (not a salesperson).

Along the way, I also learned perhaps the most important lesson in my own life. I learned that God is in control. And when you figure that out, life becomes much easier. When it's about something bigger than you and you run your business from a position of service, life is so much more enjoyable. Why worry when God is in control?

What Happens Next is Up to You

Look, I know that some of the things I've shared in this book might seem scary. Paying your team more, adding another doctor, building a new location, changing your hours, or even getting rid of patients who treat your staff poorly. These are big decisions, and they can be scary when you don't know if they'll work out.

But that's exactly why I spent so much time on metrics in this book. When you have the numbers, those scary decisions become a lot less scary. All of a sudden, you move from making decisions based on emotions and gut feelings—just hoping things will work out—to feeling confident you've made the right choice because the numbers work. And if things don't work out as planned, you can use the numbers to adjust course.

When our new Greeneville office turned out to be $7,000 more per month, we didn't panic and shut everything down. We also didn't get into a fight with our builder over it. We just went back to my spreadsheets and ran the new numbers. We were then able to figure out several options to move forward, and we could go back to our builder with ideas on how to proceed that will work for all of us.

That's the power of having good data. I can rest easy at night knowing that situation is going to work out because whatever we decide to do, we're going to do it based on the numbers. We aren't going to have to worry about whether it will work out or not! The only emotion I'm feeling about that new office is excitement.

If there was one lesson I'd want you to take from this book, it's that the courage you need to transform your practice doesn't come from being fearless. It comes from having the knowledge and data to make decisions with confidence. It comes from understanding that you get what you put into your team. It comes from knowing how to talk to your patients in a way that builds trust instead of just trying to sell them stuff. And it comes from trusting that when you're doing the right things for the right reasons, things have a way of working out.

You already have everything you need to build the practice you want. You just need to start taking action.

Your Action Plan

If you're feeling overwhelmed by everything we've covered, that's okay. You don't have to implement everything at once. In fact, I don't recommend you try to do that because you'll just end up frustrated.

Instead, I recommend using what I call the 30/60/90 plan, based on the impact/effort matrix. The idea is simple: prioritize your actions based on two factors—impact and effort required. I've included templates on the following pages to get you thinking about this.

Now, if you're like me, you probably have a lot of ideas floating around in your head. Maybe you've even been writing things down as you read. Now is the time to get those ideas out of your head and onto the page! I would highly recommend jotting down whatever ideas come to mind as you read through the following templates.

(I know some people don't like writing in books, so if you'd prefer to fill these out on your computer or print them out, you can download PDF versions at www.DrKurtSteele.com.)

30-DAY ACTIONS (HIGH IMPACT + LOW EFFORT)

These are the quick wins that will make a real difference in your practice.

Examples:

- Start tracking your revenue per exam and revenue per doctor day
- Implement the "Start With Why" approach in your patient conversations
- Begin using the herd theory when making recommendations
- Set up a system to track missed phone calls
- *(Or whatever you feel is most important for your practice!)*

Your High Impact + Low Effort Actions:

- _______________________________________
- _______________________________________
- _______________________________________
- _______________________________________
- _______________________________________
- _______________________________________
- _______________________________________
- _______________________________________

Pick 2 to Implement in the Next 30 Days!

1. _______________________________________
2. _______________________________________

60-DAY ACTIONS (MEDIUM IMPACT + LOW EFFORT)
*These changes will help, but they're not as urgent as the
30-day items.*

Examples:
- Create a written policy for family and friend discounts
- Implement reminder calls and texts to reduce no-shows
- Start using the "When were you thinking of coming in?" phone script
- Begin tracking one of the silent killers in your practice
- *(Or whatever you feel is most important for your practice!)*

Your Medium Impact + Low Effort Actions:

- _______________________________________
- _______________________________________
- _______________________________________
- _______________________________________
- _______________________________________
- _______________________________________
- _______________________________________
- _______________________________________

Pick 2 to Implement in the Next 60 Days!

1. _______________________________________
2. _______________________________________

90-DAY ACTIONS (HIGH IMPACT + HIGH EFFORT)

These are the big moves that will transform your practice, but they take more time and effort to implement properly.

Examples:

- Restructure your team's roles and give raises tied to new responsibilities
- Implement the bonus system for your team
- Establish the System of Accountability
- Review and restructure your hours to better serve your team and patients
- *(Or whatever you feel is most important for your practice!)*

Your High Impact + High Effort Actions:

- _______________________________________
- _______________________________________
- _______________________________________
- _______________________________________
- _______________________________________
- _______________________________________
- _______________________________________
- _______________________________________

Pick 2 to Implement in the Next 90 Days!

1. _______________________________________
2. _______________________________________

DON'T DO (LOW IMPACT + HIGH EFFORT)
If something falls into this category, just skip it.
(Your time and energy are too valuable to waste on things that
won't move the needle!)

Write them down:

____

____

____

____

____

____

____

____

____

The beauty of this approach is that you're constantly making progress, and it's not overwhelming. In 30 days, you'll have two wins under your belt. In 60 days, you'll have four. And in 90 days, you'll have implemented six meaningful changes in your practice. That's not a complete transformation, but it's a solid foundation to build on.

Once you've completed your two action items in each area, you can go back to your to-do list and choose another two. That way, you can keep making progress as efficiently as possible by prioritizing the ideas that provide the greatest impact for the least amount of effort.

Remember that small changes compound into massive results over time. You probably know the value of compounding interest, and the same idea applies to your business. When I started tracking my metrics for the first time back in 1998, I didn't suddenly become a business genius overnight. But over time, having those numbers helped me make better decisions, avoid costly mistakes, and grow with confidence instead of fear. That meant I was making gradual improvements that eventually compounded into big gains.

For example, when I started asking patients more questions and explaining "why" before I did anything, I didn't magically double my revenue per exam in one month. But after a year of consistent progress, that shift in how I communicated added $32 to my revenue per exam, which translated to $200,000 in additional revenue. Small changes can generate big results!

The Practice You Really Want

Before we part ways, I want you to do something for me. Close your eyes for a second and imagine your ideal practice—the one you *really* want.

What does it look like? Are you working three days a week or five? Are you booked out two months in advance or two weeks in advance? Do you have a team that's been with you for years, or are you constantly training new people? Are you making enough money to live the life you want outside of work?

Are you excited to walk through that back door every morning, or are you dreading it?

Whatever that vision looks like for you, I want you to know that it's possible. I'm living proof of that. I went from working five to six days per week and barely breaking a million in revenue to averaging three days a week across two locations, generating millions. I have team members who have been with me for over 10 years. I take multiple vacations every year. My patients love coming to see us. My team loves coming to work.

And I'm not special. I'm just a guy from Newport, Tennessee, who figured out that there's a better way to run an optometry practice—and it's not for sale!

You can build the practice you want. You just need the right information, the right systems, and the courage to make some changes. This book has given you the information and the systems. The courage? Well, that part is inside of you right now. You've always had it; just need to embrace it. Everything we've discussed up to this point should help you do that.

Just remember: When you focus on serving your team and patients well, the rest has a way of falling into place. Remembering Psalm 27:1 always helps me!

One Last Thing

I have to share one last thing that has helped me on a personal level. I know this might not be relevant to everyone, and that's okay—but hopefully you can take something from this based on whatever belief system you follow.

As I've built my practice and faced many of those tough decisions, I have found it immensely helpful to know that God is ultimately in control. Once I truly understood that, it changed everything. Knowing the metrics and having the data gives me the courage to make tough decisions. But knowing God is in control gives me an extra boost of courage, and that makes everything less stressful and overwhelming. The way I look at it, God wants me to have the energy to serve Him, to be there for my family, and to live a full life. If I can just focus on doing that, and I continue to make decisions based on that, then He will handle the rest.

Why did this have such an impact on me? Because it meant I no longer had to carry the weight of everything on my shoulders. I can make decisions knowing that as long as I operate from a place of service and do right by my team and my patients, He will handle the rest. Now, that doesn't mean I can disregard the numbers or that the decisions I make don't matter. You've clearly seen that is not how I approach things! It just means I can do all of this without the added anxiety of thinking it all depends on me. That has helped me a lot, and perhaps you can find something within your own belief system that provides a similar benefit.

With that said, I hope you've learned something (or ideally, a lot!) from this book. I know now that I spent too many years grinding away at something that should have been enjoyable. Please don't make the same mistakes I did. Don't wait for a tragedy to make you realize that life's too short to be exhausted all the time. Don't keep doing things the way you've always done them just because that's what you think success looks like.

Take what you've learned in this book and use it! Start tracking those metrics. Invest in your team. Learn to talk to your patients in a way that builds trust. Fix those silent killers. Make data-driven decisions with confidence. And remember that when you're working from a place of service and doing right by your team and patients, you don't have to carry the weight of it all on your shoulders.

You can build the practice you actually want to work at. And together, we can keep optometry independent. Together, we can build something that can compete with the big chains and corporate optometry! We are proving that independent optometry won't just survive—it will thrive.

Now get out there and make it happen. I'm rooting for you.
- Kurt

P.S. If you want to dive deeper into any of these topics or you need help implementing these strategies in your practice, visit my website at www.DrKurtSteele.com. I've got downloadable spreadsheet templates, additional resources, and information about my coaching services. And if you ever find yourself in Newport, Tennessee, stop by our office. I'd love to meet you and hear about your journey.

Acknowledgments

This book exists because of the many incredible people who have shaped my life and career. One of my reasons for writing this book was simply to tell the world about them through the stories and lessons they've taught me. If I've been able to get even one percent of the wisdom they've shared with me into this book, then I've accomplished my mission.

To Sacha, my wife—you are my heart, my soul, and my everything. They say behind every successful man is an extraordinary woman, but that phrase doesn't even come close to capturing what you mean to me and what you have done for me. You are not behind me at all! You are beside me and in many instances my leader. You are a part of every achievement I have and have reached for.

While I have been at conferences, meetings, and other practices chasing my dreams, you have been the architect of our lives. You handle all the details. You have made our house a home, and you have done it with a selflessness and grace that takes my breath away. You don't just do that for me, either. You are the best friend someone could have. I see you are the happiest when you make others happy. That is you to the core. You take care of details so people can be happy, and you do it without any need for recognition. Your selflessness has allowed me to chase very wild dreams. You are truly amazing.

You are as beautiful on the inside as you are on the outside, though even that feels like an understatement. Your selflessness humbles me daily. Your strength sustains me. Your love transforms me. I would not be where I am or *who* I am without you.

I've often said that when you marry the girl of your dreams, all your other dreams come true. Sacha, you were my first dream, my best dream, and every success in these pages exists because you made it possible for me to reach for them. Every principle about building something meaningful, every lesson about putting people first, every insight about creating something that matters—I learned it first from watching how you love. This book, this journey, and this life would mean nothing without you to share it with.

To my Mom—You taught me that "can't never could," and every time I faced something that seemed impossible, I heard your voice pushing me forward. You never let me settle for less than my best, not because you demanded perfection, but because you genuinely believed I could do anything.

You showed me that the highest calling in life is to be a best friend, and you modeled that every single day. Your friends knew that no matter what crisis hit, what time it was, or how far they were, you'd be there.

In over 56 years of being your son, you never hurt me. Not once. Not physically, not emotionally, not even for a second. 56 years of interactions, decisions, conversations, discipline, guidance, and not one moment where you made me feel small, unloved, or disappointed. Not one harsh word I had to forgive or bad action I had to overlook. I never went to bed hurt by something you said or did. That is remarkable. That is what unconditional love really means.

You created a life where I was completely safe with you and gave me the gift of never having to heal from my mother's words or actions. That's the gold standard you set, and it's the one I try to meet every day. To be someone who builds up and never tears down. To be the cheerleader who also happens to be the best friend. To love in a way that leaves no wounds, only wisdom.

To my Dad's widow, Tonya—you gave my father the greatest gift anyone could give: the ability to live his final years with dignity, at home, surrounded by love. When ALS took so much from him, you made sure it never took his comfort or his peace. You took amazing care of him and taught me what it meant to be an amazing spouse. I will always love you for the care you showed my Dad.

To my current partners, Dr. Emily Eisenhower, thank you for "coming home" and joining our practice. Thank you for being pretty much the best decision we ever made for our Newport practice. You have continued the excellent tradition started by Nathan, Bill, and Jeff. I know they are proud. You are a big reason for our success, and you replaced me as the youngest president ever of the Tennessee Association of Optometric Physicians. Most importantly, thank you for your friendship. **Dr. Graham Taylor**, Jeff was right when he hand-picked you. What you, Gloria, and our team in Greeneville have done is remarkable! You guys have really done a lot of this yourselves. I am looking forward to your book!

To Dr. Nathan Ford (who started the practice) **and Dr. Bill Henry** (who was there before Foster)—Thank you for your contributions to building something special. This practice was so well respected when I got here, it gave me a great platform to grow. I can never thank you guys enough.

To Dr. Jacob Norris—thank you for "coming home" and caring so much about our practice. You have continued the high standard of excellence set by those before us, and it is an honor to practice with you every day.

To Molly Wilson—thank you for having the courage to go from a part-time college student worker to an incredible office manager! Thank you for your leadership!

To Amie Perryman—thank you for working side by side with me for 26 years! That is amazing, and you are a big part of why we have grown so much!

To the rest of my team—Brandi Crum, Heather Hooper, Chasity Cabe, Ralonna McCarter, Jessica Bible, Jensen Van Stratum, Calley Fancher, Stephanie Clevenger (thank you for running the optical so well...a very hard job!), Erika Helton, Julia Spencer, and Brandy Avera. Y'all make me look good every single day, and I couldn't do it without you. You are just not my team, you're my family. You know I mean that.

My sister-in-law, Heather Ward, who took great care of my brother and made him the happiest I have ever seen him while adding years to his life.

To the Johnson and Spikes family, for their support through all of that. In particular, the Johnson family, who are a bunch of Ohio State and Clemson fans, but showed up to Jason's funeral in Tennessee orange just to put a smile on my face. I have an amazing family, and I am blessed.

To my Greeneville team—Gloria Coffman (our leader in Greeneville, thank you for your leadership!), Natasha Tyree, Allison Greene, Brooke Woods, Hannah Knight, Toni Laws, and Haley Luttrell, thank you for your continued excellence!

To the many past team members who helped build this practice for many years—Annette Berney (and her husband Donn), Judy Pound, Rhonda Bergin, and Emily Ellison. Thank you for all you did for our practice. Emily Ellison was the first in our practice to really learn a lot of optical and technical things to free up Jeff and me to be in the exam room. And especially to my East Tennessee Mama, Annette, I could not have done it without you. The amount of respect you had in our community and the way you were a "walking Rolodex" and knew every single person that came in that door—not just their name, but all about them—was just amazing. You were a big part of our growth, and I could not have done that without you. I miss you every day.

To the First Baptist Church of Newport, Tennessee, my pastor, Rich Lloyd, our church leaders, Rob Myers, Rebekah Fisher, Travis Hall, and my Sunday school class (especially my teachers, David Kickliter, Doug Shoemaker, and Terry Capshaw)—Thank you for that sense of community and family that comes from worshipping He who created us. We have a lot of great times together, and I truly look forward to learning from y'all every Sunday. I learn from everyone in that class, and I have a lot of great examples of how to be a Christian man that I follow every day. Y'all have no idea how much you mean to me. God bless each one of you!

To Mark B. Murphy—my financial advisor for over 15 years and so much more than that. Your advice has shaped not just my portfolio, but my entire approach to building wealth with purpose. From strategy sessions to those incredible third-row seats at MSG watching the Knicks, you've shown me that the best business relationships become real friendships. Thank you for being a mentor who taught me that financial success without personal fulfillment is bankruptcy by another name. Thanks for being in my corner, Mark, both in business and as a friend.

To Amber Vilhauer (No Guts, No Glory)—thank you for being the guide I didn't know I needed. You kept me aligned when my thoughts scattered, on track when life pulled me sideways, and focused when the blank page felt overwhelming. More than teaching me how to write a book, you taught me how to truly listen—to let others be heard before rushing to be understood. You transformed how I lead, how I speak, and how I connect. This book exists because you believed in its message before I could fully articulate it. You coached me through every doubt. I couldn't have done this without you, Amber. Thank you for helping me find my voice while teaching me to honor others' voices, too.

To Aidan Diprima—thank you for going so far above and beyond the call of duty in writing this book. My ADHD can be hard to deal with, and you took every change and suggestion with such grace and patience! I could not have done this without you.

To my Vision Source family—Thank you for your guidance, mentorship, and for creating a community that elevates all of us. Joining Vision Source was one of the defining moments of my career, as it is for so many other optometrists. It is amazing what I have learned at all the local, regional, and national meetings that have grown my practice. Not to mention all of the email threads and information on our portal full of ideas to help with our success. To me, Vision Source is crucial in making sure independent optometry continues to thrive in the future.

To everyone at the Tennessee Association of Optometric Physicians (TAOP)—thank you for your leadership and for fighting for our profession.

To the Southern College of Optometry—thank you for preparing me to serve patients well.

To everyone I've mentioned here: you've made my life richer and my work more meaningful. This book is a small way of saying thank you.

My beautiful wife, Sacha!

In Memoriam

My mom and Jason

Me and Jason as kids! A long time ago.

In Memory of My Brother, Jason Steele.

You taught me about true loyalty. The kind that exists only between brothers who truly love each other.

There's something irreplaceable about a sibling you're completely safe with. With Jason, there was no performance, no filter, no fear of judgment. We could say the most ridiculous things, share our worst thoughts, admit our biggest failures, and somehow it would all end in laughter. I miss that every day. Not just the laughter, but the freedom to be completely myself with someone so close.

You were my vault, Jason. I could discuss every secret, worry, and wild idea with you, knowing they were safe. You never once used them against me or made me feel small. To the world, I had to show up as Dr. Steele, the business owner, optometrist, coach, and leader. But with you, I could just be

Kurt. I wasn't always right, and I wasn't always strong, I was always your brother, and that's all that mattered to us.

We had each other's backs without question, and that is something I will never forget. Of all the losses, losing you cut the deepest. You were so much more than a brother—you were my safe place, my reality check, my guaranteed laugh when I needed one most. Every day, I find myself wanting to call you with something only you would understand or find funny. Something only a brother could hear. That's the hardest part.

You taught me that loyalty is about being the person someone can trust with their whole truth. Besides Sacha, you were that person for me, Jason. You always will be.

In Memory of My Dad, Steve Steele.

You taught me that success is measured in lives touched and people who feel seen. You drove four hours to support a new pastor in our family, not because you had to, but because showing up mattered. You made that five-hour drive every Tuesday and Friday to watch me play basketball, even though we both knew I'd never make the NBA. You taught me about loyalty, presence, and the kind of love that shows up regardless of the scoreboard.

You had this gift for finding the person standing alone at the edge of the room. There were so many stories at your funeral about how you made those people feel like they were the most important person in the room. You taught me that leadership isn't about being the loudest voice; it's about making sure every voice feels heard.

Your business wisdom shaped everything I do today. You showed me the true value of generosity and going the extra mile. You taught me why data matters, and you proved that putting people first makes everything better. Most importantly, you lived out your belief that you can't outgive God. I saw how you gave to others, and it came back multiplied. I've spent my life trying to prove you right—in my practice, in my partnerships, in every decision I make, I hear your voice reminding me that the best investment is always in people.

Dr. Foster and Annette Berney

In Memory of My Brother, Mentor, and Friend, Dr. Jeff Foster.

Five years have passed since we lost you. There isn't a day I don't think about what you'd say about where we've taken the practice, what joke you'd make about our latest venture (like your classic introduction, "this is Kurt, and he is costing me a lot of money!"), or how you'd somehow make even the biggest challenges seem manageable with your wisdom and that laugh of yours. By the way, I also remember how you would end that introduction with, "And he has made me a lot more money!"

They voted you Tennessee OD of the Decade in 2015, and it wasn't even the end of a decade—we had simply run out of awards to give you. That was you, Jeff. You didn't fit into normal categories or timelines. You were larger than life, and you made everyone around you better just by being who you were. You certainly made optometry better. I don't think there is any doubt you are on the Mount Rushmore of Tennessee Optometry.

I became Tennessee president at thirty-one years old for one reason: I was Jeff Foster's practice partner. Every door that opened, every opportunity that came, every ounce of credibility I had in those early years—it all came from standing next to you. I was just smart enough to hang on to your coattails and pay attention.

But we were more than senior and junior partners. We were brothers. Our trust didn't come from contracts or agreements—it was built on countless hours working side by side, on shared dreams of what independent optometry could be, and having a blast during every minute of that journey. We hardly ever had a cross word, did we?! Except for that one time I thought you should be paid more than me, and you didn't want to take it! That trust is what allowed us to take a small practice and transform it into something neither of us could have built alone.

I wish you could see what Vision Source of Newport and Greeneville has become. Actually, I take that back—somehow, I think you do see it. And I hope you're proud.

This one's for you, brother. Thank you for believing in a young OD who had no business thinking he could do what we did. Thank you for showing me what real leadership looks like. Thank you for being the kind of partner who made work feel like purpose and partnership feel like family.

Until we meet again,

Kurt

www.ingramcontent.com/pod-product-compliance
Lightning Source LLC
Chambersburg PA
CBHW030859060726